MW01096621

Creating the Future
of Faculty Development

Creating the Future of Faculty Development

Learning From the Past,
Understanding the Present

Mary Deane Sorcinelli
University of Massachusetts Amherst

Ann E. Austin
Michigan State University

Pamela L. Eddy
Central Michigan University

Andrea L. Beach
Western Michigan University

ANKER PUBLISHING COMPANY, INC.
Bolton, Massachusetts

Creating the Future of Faculty Development
Learning From the Past, Understanding the Present

ISBN 1-882982-87-8

Composition and cover design by Jessica Holland

Anker Publishing Company, Inc.
563 Main Street
P.O. Box 249
Bolton, MA 01740-0249 USA

www.ankerpub.com

Library of Congress Cataloging-in-Publication Data

Creating the future of faculty development : learning from the past, understanding the present / Mary Deane Sorcinelli ... [et al].
    p. cm.
  Includes bibliographical references and index.
  ISBN 1-882982-87-8
  1. Universities and colleges—Faculty. 2. College teachers—Professional relationships. 3. College teachers—In-service training. I. Sorcinelli, Mary Deane.

  LB2331.7.C74 2006
  378.1'25—dc22

                    2005015282

About the Authors

Mary Deane Sorcinelli is associate provost for faculty development, director of the Center for Teaching, and an associate professor in the Department of Educational Policy, Research, and Administration at the University of Massachusetts Amherst. Her research and publications concern academic career development, teaching improvement and evaluation, and faculty development policy and practice. She served as president on the executive board of the Professional and Organizational Development Network in Higher Education from 2000–2004. She was a visiting scholar to the American Association for Higher Education from 1999–2001, and is currently a Whiting Foundation Fellow, studying faculty and teaching development practices in Ireland (2003–2005). Her books include *Evaluation of Teaching Handbook* (1986, Indiana University–Bloomington), *Academic Memories: Retired Faculty Members Recall the Past* (1988, Western Sun), *Developing New and Junior Faculty* (coedited with A. Austin, 1992, Jossey-Bass), *Writing to Learn: Strategies for Assigning and Responding to Writing Across the Disciplines* (coedited with P. Elbow, 1997, Jossey-Bass), *Preparing a Teaching Portfolio* (with F. Mues, 2000, Center for Teaching, University of Massachusetts Amherst), and *Heeding New Voices: Academic Careers for a New Generation* (with R. E. Rice & A. Austin, 2000, American Association for Higher Education).

Ann E. Austin is professor in the Higher, Adult, and Lifelong Education Program at Michigan State University. Her research and publications concern faculty careers, roles, and professional development; teaching and learning issues in higher education; and organizational change and transformation in higher education. She was a Fulbright Fellow in South Africa (1998), the president of the Association for the Study of Higher Education (2001–2002), and is currently co-principle investigator of a National Science Foundation Center concerning preparing future faculty in STEM (Science, Technology, Engineering, Mathematics) fields. Her books include *Paths to the Professoriate: Strategies for Enriching the Preparation of Future Faculty* (coedited with D. H. Wulff, 2004, Jossey-Bass), *Higher Education in the Developing World: Changing Contexts and Institutional Resources* (coedited with D. W. Chapman, 2002, Greenwood Press), *Heeding New Voices: Academic Careers for a New Generation* (with R. E. Rice & M. D. Sorcinelli, 2000, American Association for Higher Education), and *Developing New and Junior Faculty* (coedited with M. D. Sorcinelli, 1992, Jossey-Bass).

Pamela L. Eddy is an assistant professor of higher education at Central Michigan University. She serves as an associate editor for *Community College Enterprise* and is incoming book review coeditor for the *Community College Journal of Research and Practice*. She is a board member of Division J of the American Education Research Association and a board representative for the Council for the Study of Community Colleges. Her research concerns leadership and faculty development at community colleges, new faculty roles, and teaching and learning issues.

Andrea L. Beach is an assistant professor in teaching, learning, and leadership at Western Michigan University, where she teaches in the higher education leadership doctoral program. She received her Ph.D. in higher, adult, and lifelong education from Michigan State University as well as her master's in adult and continuing education. Her research centers on issues of organizational climate in universities, teaching and learning, doctoral education, and faculty development. Recent projects include a national survey of community college faculty development, a national survey of faculty development at Historically Black Colleges and Universities, and creation of a compilation of online teaching. She is currently external evaluator on three grants addressing faculty development and faculty learning communities.

Table of Contents

Preface

The 21st century has introduced a host of new challenges to American colleges and universities. The external environment has become more complicated and demanding. Parents, employers, donors, boards of trustees, and government leaders increasingly raise questions about the role of higher education institutions in society and demand evidence of outcomes from investment of public and private resources. Universities and colleges feel pressure to address and balance multiple missions: knowledge dissemination through teaching, knowledge production through research, and knowledge application through service and outreach projects that link institutional expertise with societal problems. Among institutions there is intensified competition for faculty, students, research grants, revenue, and prestige. Universities and colleges also face a changing internal environment—the increasing use of information technologies, the steady growth in diversity of the student body, and an emergent focus on interdisciplinary programs.

As faculty members and faculty developers with more than 50 combined years of experience in higher education, we believe that faculty development is a key strategic lever for ensuring institutional quality and supporting institutional change. This study combines findings about the purposes, issues, and preferences of current faculty developers as well as their assessment of the challenges confronting higher education institutions. We also offer our thoughts on an emerging agenda. Our goal is to help both developers and institutions prepare for the future.

As this book was going to press the American Association for Higher Education announced that it would cease operations after almost 40 years of serving all those interested in higher education issues and educational practices, especially teaching, learning, assessment, and faculty roles and rewards. The loss of this important resource underscores the need for all of us in the higher education community to consider the challeges that face us as we look to the years ahead.

We would like to thank our colleagues in the Professional and Organizational Development Network in Higher Education (POD Network), both American and Canadian, for their participation in our study and for their informed and thoughtful insights. Special thanks to the executive director of the POD Network, Kay Herr Gillespie, for her constructive comments on an early draft. We also thank the developers in the Historically Black Colleges and Universities Faculty Development Network and the National Council for Staff, Program, and Organizational Development community college developers who are currently taking our survey. They will further extend the diversity of perspectives on faculty development found in this book.

It would be impossible to thank all of our colleagues in our respective teaching and learning centers and academic departments for their advice and encouragement. There are, however, two people that we would like to thank individually. Jung Yun, a graduate student at the University of Massachusetts Amherst, deserves our enduring gratitude for her patient review of draft after draft—suggesting and making changes, checking and updating references. Mary Bellino was invaluable in helping to bring the book-writing process to conclusion. She organized and painstakingly edited the final draft, and the book is improved immeasurably by her input. We also thank Jim Anker and Carolyn Dumore at Anker Publishing—their expertise was invaluable at every stage of the writing and production of this book. Finally, we would like to thank our families. They have been supportive and patient, and we are grateful.

Mary Deane Sorcinelli
Ann E. Austin
Pamela L. Eddy
Andrea L. Beach
April 2005

Re-envisioning Faculty and Faculty Development

At the heart of the university or college are its faculty members—the men and women who devote their lives to the research, teaching, and service missions of higher education institutions. Many would agree that the quality of a university or college, though influenced by numerous factors, is related most closely to the work of the faculty. Their expertise, commitment, energy, and creativity directly shape the experiences of students, the nature of research, and the impact of the institution on the broader community.

For several decades, many higher education institutions have recognized the value of faculty development—some form of organized support to help faculty members develop as teachers, scholars, and citizens of their campuses, professions, and broader communities. Approaches to faculty development have evolved over the past 40 years in response to changing external expectations for higher education institutions and changing faculty needs. (It should be noted that although some new terminology to describe the field is emerging, such as *academic development* and *educational development*, we have chosen to use the more commonly accepted term *faculty development*.)

Over the decades, many institutions have established centers, committees, or other structures to manage faculty development activities. At the same time, faculty development has become a professional field in which individuals acquire specific skills for supporting the professional growth of faculty colleagues. As described in Chapter 1, the first professional organization for faculty developers in North America, the Professional and Organizational Development Network in Higher Education (POD Network), was established in 1974 and has grown steadily in membership as well as in the number of publications, conferences, workshops, and other resources it offers. In addition, other higher education organizations such as the American Association for Higher Education (AAHE), scholarly organizations such as the American Sociological Association (ASA), and accrediting organizations such as the Middle States Association of Schools and Colleges (MSA) have recognized that faculty development plays an important part in promoting and disseminating effective educational practices.

Efforts to support and enrich faculty work—particularly in a changing context—are critically important to faculty members, institutional leaders, and higher education itself. In this book we explore how faculty development evolved over time, take a snapshot of current faculty development in American colleges and universities, and then offer a vision for the future of faculty development. Specifically, this book addresses several key questions:

- What are the structural variations among faculty development programs?
- What goals, purposes, and models guide and influence program development?
- What are the top challenges facing faculty members, institutions, and faculty development programs?
- What are potential new directions and visions for the field of faculty development?

To set the stage for our exploration of these issues, we begin by explaining more fully why we have written this book and how it is organized.

I   The Need to Review and Enlarge the Vision of Faculty Development

The increasing complexity of the external environment plays a significant role in the current period of challenge and change in higher education. Everyone, from parents to legislators, expects institutions of higher education to assure measurable outcomes, to adequately prepare graduates to engage in meaningful work and be productive members of the workplace, to spend resources wisely, and to fulfill the public trust historically bestowed upon them. Competition to respond to these demands is escalating among traditional institutions, while at the same time the number of for-profit, virtual, and online universities and colleges continues to grow.

In response to public demands, market forces, and their own commitment to excellence, higher education institutions are attending more closely to each of their missions. For example, in terms of teaching, faculty members are facing instructional situations in which students may differ widely in their levels of interest and commitment, their preparation, their availability for course-related work, and their learning styles. The ethnic and social diversity in the classroom is also changing as enrollments of women, multicultural, and minority students continue to increase. Attention to diversity and multiculturalism is high on the agenda of many colleges and universities; helping faculty members to develop more inclusive course materials and teaching methods has thus become an important goal for many campuses. Institutions aim to provide other kinds of academic support, since with rapid technological advances faculty members are now called on to provide responsive, low-cost educational opportunities and to develop educational delivery in new formats—through web sites, short modules, and certificate programs. Many faculty members have not been trained to teach in these new contexts, and although their specific needs may vary, they require support and training to function optimally in a rapidly changing technological environment. In addition, faculty are being asked to assess and evaluate student learning outcomes (Angelo & Cross, 1993), make teaching more public (Shulman, 2000), and study and document their own teaching (Hutchings, 2000; Hutchings & Shulman, 1999).

Furthermore, in many fields there is a growing recognition and acceptance of new ways of understanding and conducting research—what Lincoln (1999) calls the emergence of "postmodern understandings." Closely related is the blurring of traditional boundaries between disciplines and fields. Faculty members are becoming engaged in cross-disciplinary or multidisciplinary work, framing questions in new ways, using methodologies in which they were not originally trained, and seeking out deeper expertise in new knowledge domains (Lattuca, 2002). As faculty members pursue new scholarly interests, the cost of doing research and the competition for federal and foundation-sponsored research and development dollars continue to escalate.

Finally, at a number of institutions, faculty members have been encouraged to become more engaged scholars, linking their research more closely with problems in the local, national, or international community. For example, the increase in service-learning as an integral part of undergraduate education provides a forum for students to address community problems and for faculty members to tie their research to these problems. Thus faculty require new skills for engaging with the needs and concerns of constituencies on and off campus, in skillfully communicating a range of ideas to diverse audiences, and in documenting how their time is allocated.

The demographics of the faculty are also shifting. Between the end of World War II and the early 1970s the number of college and university professors tripled, the most rapid growth occurring during the 1960s (Altbach, 1994). The 1970s and 1980s were a time of constrained mobility and hiring; faculty development was seen as one way to help maintain professors' vitality during a period of retrenchment. Now, many faculty members hired in the post–World War II boom are retiring, and for the first time in decades, higher education institutions must replace a substantial portion of the professoriate. A significant trend in higher education employment patterns is the dramatic increase in the number of part-time faculty and the number of full-time, off-tenure-track term appointments (Baldwin & Chronister, 2001;

Finkelstein & Schuster, 2001; Finkelstein, Seal, & Schuster, 1998; Gappa & Leslie, 1993, 1997). Universities and colleges must be prepared to help these new colleagues—both those in traditional positions and those in term and part-time appointments—succeed in their professional roles.

In sum, major forces in the external and internal environment are transforming our institutions of higher education. Faculty members face new challenges: the demands by legislators, employers, and parents for assessment and accountability; the call for the academy to embrace an increasingly diverse student body and to serve as an exemplar of how multiculturalism can become the basis for institutional and societal strength; the possibilities introduced by new technologies and the parallel expectations by many students and employers that universities and colleges will utilize these technologies in creative ways; and the trend in higher education toward community outreach and problem solving at every level—from local to global.

All of these changes are occurring in the face of increased competition and a tightening of resources at higher education institutions, and at a time when faculty ranks are being replenished with new colleagues. Faculty development is needed more than ever, but the ways in which faculty development has been conceptualized at many institutions over the past few decades may not fully meet the array of challenges facing the professoriate today. Systems thinkers, such as Senge (1990), argue that effective organizations must be "learning organizations" in which participants constantly engage in reflection, adaptation, and growth. Others have observed that while industries invest much in research and development, higher education organizations historically have focused much less attention internally on providing resources to enhance and expand the talents of their faculty.

In this changing context, universities and colleges require committed, competent, energetic, and effective faculty members who can respond to multiple expectations, engage in revenue-producing activities, and maintain the highest level of quality in their work. Faculty development thus becomes essential to both the individual faculty member and the higher education institution as a whole. To meet shifting expectations for which they may not be fully prepared, faculty may need academic support systems and professional learning opportunities beyond those traditionally offered. Providing institutional support for faculty members facing changing contexts and new demands becomes an essential strategic choice. We believe that the contours of change require us to rethink how we approach, organize, and support faculty development.

Organization of the Book

Our purpose in writing this book is to consider the future of faculty development in ways that will engage both new and experienced developers. We begin by recalling the past. Chapter 1 provides a retrospective of faculty development. How has it been traditionally conceptualized and organized, and what have been its goals, practices, and outcomes? We discuss the first four ages of faculty development and introduce the era we inhabit now, which we call the Age of the Network. In Chapter 2, we turn to a snapshot of faculty development as it is currently practiced. Drawing on a study we conducted in 2001–2002, we examine the demographics of faculty developers and the structures and goals of existing programs. Chapter 3 identifies the organizations, literatures, and faculty development programs that influence the work of faculty developers. Chapter 4 surveys important issues in teaching, learning, and faculty work that developers currently address—or do not address—in their programs.

In Chapter 5 we turn to the future, describing the new challenges and pressures on faculty members and higher education institutions that will continue to affect faculty work. We also identify top challenges that faculty development professionals believe can be addressed through faculty development. Chapter 6 presents an overview and sample of developers' responses to our survey's two open-ended questions about the future of faculty development. Chapter 7 offers a vision of what faculty development might become. It should be noted that all of the chapters examine the important differences in the responses of developers from different institutional types (community colleges, liberal arts colleges, comprehensives, and research/doctoral universities) to questions about how faculty development *is* and *should be* conceptualized. We use quotes from developers' open-ended comments on the survey throughout the chapters to illustrate and illuminate key findings. We also highlight award-winning programs that have been responsive to leading issues and challenges.

Faculty development is essential for the success of both individual faculty members and the institution as a whole. We hope that our findings will further encourage universities and colleges to give faculty development a central role in relation to strategic institutional planning, management, and leadership.

1

The Evolution of
Faculty Development

Faculty development is not a new phenomenon in the history of higher education. The oldest support for faculty development, the sabbatical leave, began at Harvard University in 1810 (Eble & McKeachie, 1985) and has enjoyed a long tenure. In fact, sabbaticals, leaves, and other means of advancing scholarship remained almost the exclusive form of faculty development until the 1970s. Since that time, the field has expanded to include a much broader range of concerns. As early as 1976, faculty development was defined as "the total development of the faculty member—as a person, as a professional and as a member of an academic community" (Crow, Milton, Moomaw, & O'Connell, 1976, p. 3). But fulfilling the goal of "total development" has been an ongoing challenge as the field has worked to broaden its horizons and meet the expectations set for it.

In this chapter, we first review the general history of faculty development and its growth as a profession, then trace the evolution of the goals, practices, and structures that have characterized faculty development from its inception to the present day. Finally, we summarize the studies that have had a significant effect on the field. We divide the earlier history of faculty development into four ages: the Age of the Scholar, the Age of the Teacher, the Age of the Developer, and the Age of the Learner. As we enter the current age, which we call the Age of the Network, the emphases, interconnections, and contradictions among the four earlier ages will help us to envision the future of faculty development.

The Five Ages

From the mid-1950s well into the 1960s, American higher education grew rapidly in size and affluence. Equally striking was the prestige and status afforded to the academic profession. For example, between 1953 and 1962, the role of professor rose from seventh to third place in Gallup polls assessing the attractiveness of nine leading professions, a rank it would hold until 1973 (Rice, 1996). In describing this expansionist period, marked by new sources of funding for programs and the rising influence of the academic scholar, Rice noted that

> institutional responsibilities such as the teaching of undergraduates and committee work could be tolerated as long as time was made for doing one's own work and support was provided; a Faustian bargain was struck. Within a relatively short period, being a scholar became virtually synonymous with being an academic professional, and a powerful image of what this meant took hold. (p. 8)

This period, then, was the Age of the Scholar, and faculty development efforts were directed almost entirely toward improving and advancing scholarly competence.

By the late 1960s and throughout the 1970s the baby boomers were heading off to college; suddenly institutions of higher education found themselves serving a much larger and broader range of students. Student activism was not only political, but also academic and focused on teaching—students demanded the right to exercise some control over the quality of their undergraduate learning experience, by such means as evaluating their teachers' performance in the classroom. At the same time, economic recession and the concomitant decline in faculty mobility and opportunities for renewal also contributed to new interest in faculty development and instructional improvement. These changes ushered in the Age of the Teacher. A seminal monograph, *Faculty Development in a Time of Retrenchment* (Astin, Comstock, Epperson, Greeley, Katz, & Kaufman, 1974), focused on teaching development as key to faculty vitality and renewal. Earlier interest in behavioristic research on college-level teaching was superseded by an interest in research and practice related to the development of teaching skills and competencies, as well as the design of teaching development and evaluation programs (Alstete, 2000).

The 1980s began the Age of the Developer; with an upsurge in faculty development programs, the profession came of age. Although this period was characterized by tight budgets and a concomitant decline in conditions of academic life (e.g., reduced travel, equipment, and personnel resources), a number of universities and colleges began new programs or rejuvenated existing ones (Eble & McKeachie, 1985; Erickson, 1986). Concerned about faculty vitality, foundations such as Bush, Ford, and Lilly assisted by making major investments in faculty development. Several national reports urging that more attention be paid to undergraduate education spurred further activity (Boyer, 1987; National Commission on Excellence in Education, 1983; Study Group on the Conditions of Excellence in American Higher Education, 1984). While some researchers continued to explore the question of who was participating in faculty development and what services were offered (Erickson, 1986), others began to study the usefulness and measurable outcomes of development activities (Clark, Corcoran, & Lewis, 1986; Eble & McKeachie, 1985; Young, 1987). The evaluation of faculty members, particularly as teachers, became a popular concept, indeed a buzzword, in the 1980s (Alstete, 2000).

The 1990s saw accelerated changes in academic work that had enormous implications for faculty development. As Austin (2002a) noted, it was a decade characterized by changing approaches to teaching and learning. Student learning rather than teaching took center stage—the teacher was no longer the "sage on the stage," pouring knowledge into empty vessels, but a "guide on the side," facilitating student learning. Student diversity, which became greater than at any other time in the history of higher education, also called for a greater range and variety in teaching and learning methods, skills, and sensitivities. If the 1970s were the Age of the Teacher, the 1990s were the Age of the Learner.

The role of new technologies, both in teaching and research, continued to evolve. There was a veritable explosion of technology use in college teaching, including presentation tools, web sites, classroom communication systems, and online courses (McKeachie, 2002). In addition, teaching and learning centers and entire campuses witnessed the growing phenomenon of assessment and performance measurement—from the individual faculty member in his or her classroom to the departmental, institutional, and state levels (Bourne, Gates, & Cofer, 2000; Ewell, 2001; Stassen & Sorcinelli, 2001).

Perhaps most dramatic was the change in faculty roles. Traditional faculty appointments became more demanding and expansive. Teaching, research, service, outreach, advising, grant-getting, and administrative duties were all part of the full-time faculty role at many universities and colleges (Rice, Sorcinelli, & Austin, 2000). At the same time, some faculty jobs became more circumscribed; these included, for example, teaching-intensive appointments in writing, foreign languages, and instructional technology, as well as clinical or extension appointments. The rise in new, nontenure-track, and part-time faculty demanded ever more attention to faculty needs as teachers and scholars (Finkelstein & Schuster, 2001).

Finally, greater competition, less funding, and the press to develop new revenues became pronounced as the 1990s ended. Particularly in public higher education, it became evident that major increases in funding would have to come from federal grants and the private sector. Both faculty and faculty developers were encouraged to do their part to raise money for their colleges and universities at a time when funding was becoming more difficult to secure and traditional sources of funding were declining.

With the new millennium faculty development has, we believe, entered a new age—the Age of the Network. Faculty, developers, and institutions alike are facing heightened expectations, and meeting these expectations will require a collaborative effort among all stakeholders in higher education. The roles of full-time tenure-track faculty are expanding and the variety of faculty appointments is increasing, as is the pressure on faculty to perform well in all roles. Institutional environments are changing both externally and internally; issues of funding and accountability can be expected to remain at the fore throughout the coming years. How faculty development can best grow and change to meet the needs of faculty and their institutions is the subject of this book. The number of developers is increasing, and research on faculty development continues to expand as well. In addition to the study on which this book is based, several other more recent studies are highlighted in the last section of this chapter. These projects, as well as the data reported in the subsequent chapters of this book, point to the variety of ways in which faculty developers and teaching and learning centers are being called on to help faculty members fulfill their many responsibilities.

Professional Organization and Recognition

As faculty development began to expand its goals and establish formal programs, it also took on a professional identity. Two national conferences were held in the early 1970s for practitioners and experts in the field, one at Kansas State University and the other at the University of Massachusetts Amherst (Blackburn, 1980). These early gatherings signaled a growing interest in faculty development as an area for study and professional focus. In 1974, the Professional and Organizational Development Network in Higher Education (POD Network) was formed. From its outset, the POD Network's purpose has been to support improvement in higher education through faculty, instructional, and organizational development activities. The POD Network has more than 1400 members—faculty and graduate student developers, faculty members, administrators, consultants, and others. It provides support and services for its members through publications and resources, grants and awards, conferences, consulting, and networking (http://www.podnetwork.org).

Three years later, in 1977, the National Council for Staff, Program, and Organizational Development (NCSPOD) was formed to provide support for community college faculty developers. Since its inception, NCSPOD has sponsored an annual conference on the "nuts and bolts" of practical solutions to development problems. Like POD, the goal of NCSPOD is to support its members via an annual conference, publications, retreats, and awards (http://www.ncspod.org).

At around the same time, a desire for a more formal structure for faculty development in Canada rose to the top of the agenda of a group of faculty development professionals. Developers from the Universities of Guelph, McMaster, Waterloo, and Western Ontario had met informally for several years to discuss teaching and learning issues. In 1981, they founded the Society for Teaching and Learning in Higher Education (STLHE) to bring together and support those individuals who were interested in the improvement of teaching and learning in higher education in Canada. STLHE sponsors an annual conference, a series of workshops and special interest groups, an electronic forum, 3M Teaching Fellowships, and a range of publications, including a newsletter (http://www.mcmaster.ca/stlhe).

During the 1980s faculty development solidified its professional base and expanded its activities. The 1990s saw a spike in interest among higher education associations and foundations in establishing programs that support the teaching roles of faculty, or faculty development. Sometimes they joined forces with centers for teaching and learning, such as in the Carnegie Academy for the Scholarship of Teaching and Learning, and sometimes they launched their own initiatives. For example, the American Association for Higher Education (AAHE), the American Association of Colleges and Universities, the American Council on Education (ACE), the Carnegie Academy for the Advancement of Teaching, the Council of Graduate Schools, the National Science Foundation, and the Woodrow Wilson Foundation have tackled issues related to faculty roles and rewards, the scholarship of teaching and learning, the preparation of graduate students and new faculty, diversity, technology, active learning, and assessment.

Similarly, the role of professional associations such as the American Historical Association and the American Assembly of Collegiate Schools of Business in supporting effective teaching and student learning increased during the 1990s. Work began at the level of academic disciplines to reconsider definitions of scholarly, creative, and intellectual contributions in order to further important work such as the development of courses and curricula, instructional software, and textbooks (Diamond & Adam, 1993).

The recognition of faculty development as a key to educational excellence was further strengthened by the Theodore M. Hesburgh Award, inaugurated in 1993. This award, sponsored by the Teachers Insurance and Annuity Association–College Retirement Equities Fund, recognizes exceptional faculty development programs that enhance undergraduate teaching and learning. The Hesburgh Award has brought national visibility to meritorious faculty development programs at a range of institutions and has encouraged programs to prove their success and impact through evidence of systemic change in teaching effectiveness and sustained faculty commitment, hard data objectively documenting improvements in teaching and learning outcomes, and results showing the program's impact on the academic community.

Finally, the 1990s marked the globalization of faculty development with the creation of several international faculty development organizations. Both the Staff and Educational Development Association (SEDA) and the International Consortium for Educational Development (ICED) were founded in England in 1993. SEDA's mission is to encourage the improvement of all aspects of learning and teaching in higher education through staff development. ICED was established to promote educational or academic development in higher education worldwide. Both organizations sponsor national and international conferences, publications, and networks. SEDA's specific aims and activities can be found at http://www.seda.ac.uk; ICED's services are detailed at a web site hosted by the University of Western Australia at http://www.osds.uwa.edu.au/about/activities/hosted_sites/iced.

In 1999 the Institute for Learning and Teaching in Higher Education (ILTHE) was launched in the United Kingdom and then transferred into a new Higher Education Academy (HEA) in 2004. Unlike the nonprofit faculty development associations typical in the United States, HEA receives direct funding from the Higher Education Funding Councils and the government. It serves as the authoritative national voice on teaching and learning issues and is designed to promote the professional development of staff through a range of services, to support the enhancement work of universities and colleges, and to stimulate and carry out research into learning and teaching. HEA news, events, publications and resources can be found on their website at http://www.heacademy.ac.uk.

Goals

The general goals of faculty development have shifted considerably over the last five decades. In the Age of the Scholar, the emphasis on research as the central professional endeavor of academic life meant that the definition and purpose of faculty development was fairly narrow—to provide opportunities for improvement and advancement in scholarship. Eble and McKeachie (1985), Rice (1996), and others noted that academics long tended to be professionals in their discipline but not necessarily professionals in teaching. Hence the key goal of professional development was to help faculty maintain currency in their disciplines and to enhance their content expertise, a goal tied to the dominant belief system about content mastery as the means for development. Tiberius (2002) characterized this belief system as one in which little could be done to improve the teaching of professors: "Teachers were expected to be the masters of their specialty and needed not be a master of teaching" (p. 22).

The emergence of faculty development programs during the Age of the Teacher reflected a realization that faculty should not only be better prepared in their disciplines, but also better able to teach. Thus the goals of improving educational quality and of sustaining the vitality of faculty members as scholars expanded to emphasize the improvement of faculty as teachers. While the faculty member as teacher was a dominant consideration of many programs, some explored other approaches such as instructional development, focused on courses and curriculum, and organizational development, focused on institutional structure and process (Diamond, 2002).

Gaff and Simpson (1994) argue that the 1980s were characterized by centers that "aimed more at meeting the multidimensional and ever-changing needs of the total faculty" rather than earlier centers that tended to "reflect a singularity of purpose" (p. 170). Indeed, Eble and McKeachie (1985) found an amazing diversity of 37 different types of faculty development programs proposed and conducted by a range of institutions supported by the Bush Foundation. If measured by participation, activities such as teaching and learning workshops and seminars were greeted with more enthusiasm than in the 1970s. During the Age of the Developer, the faculty development movement also broadened its scope to include programs responding to the career span of academic life (e.g., mid-career renewal, retirement planning programs, career counseling, and wellness programs). As Lewis (1998) notes, "faculty development moved into more holistic development activities" (p. 29). Regardless of purpose, faculty development programs were increasingly supported by institutional as well as foundation funds, received much stronger support for instruction from central administration, and were guided by the needs of faculty rather than those of a president or provost (Gaff & Simpson, 1994).

During the 1990s, the number of faculty development centers continued to grow, not only at research universities, but also at comprehensive campuses, small liberal arts colleges, and community colleges. Many centers continued to focus on teaching and learning goals and agendas—assisting instructors in understanding underlying theories of teaching and learning and in expanding their repertoire of skills and strategies in order to adapt to the educational needs of students. At the same time, the goals and priorities of centers in the 1990s reflected the new developments, fast-moving fields, and the complex, ever-changing dynamics of college teaching in the Age of the Learner. Faculty development programs were asked to anticipate and provide support for new priorities driven by increasing opportunities and challenges, such as technology, multiculturalism, and assessment. In addition, faculty development centers, national-level foundations, disciplinary organizations, and other higher education associations all encouraged a focus on rewarding good teaching and promoting best practices. These goals will continue in the Age of the Network, and how best to prioritize them will be one of the major challenges of the new century.

Practices

During the Age of the Scholar, both institutions and foundations supported the press for research and scholarly capability as the keys to professionalism and the belief in content mastery as the key to teaching. Faculty development was individual development as well. Faculty were given funding for such activities as sabbatical leaves, attending the meetings of professional associations, and completing advanced degrees. They were given paid leaves of absence for advanced study and load adjustments for research and writing. Faculty themselves perceived such conventional support for scholarship as the best means of furthering their professional development (Eble & McKeachie, 1985). One major exception was the Associates Program, established by the Danforth Foundation in 1941. It sought to improve the quality of human relations in colleges and universities by recognizing talented teachers and their spouses through grants to support individual educational projects (Mathis, 1982).

The 1970s offered a broader range of suggested activities for faculty development work, guided by the seminal frameworks outlined by Bergquist and Phillips (1975) and Gaff (1975). Bergquist and Phillips posited that effective faculty development must become an interactive process along three dimensions: organizational, instructional, and personal. *Organizational development* includes programs that create an effective institutional environment for teaching and learning, with such activities as administrative development for chairs, deans, and other academic leaders, and the establishment of policies that incorporate the evaluation and recognition of teaching into the reward structure. *Instructional development* is focused on the process of education and includes evaluating course organization, presentation skills, and effectiveness through such means as class visits, videotaping, and student feedback. Programs might address the identification of course goals and teaching methods, broader curriculum development, and media design components. *Personal development* includes programs to promote personal growth, life planning, and interpersonal skills.

Gaff's model (1975), based on an analysis of about 200 institutions, was similar, emphasizing *faculty development*, focused on the improvement of classroom teaching and learning over the career span; *instructional development*, focused on the design of courses; and *organizational development*, focused on the institutional environment that creates the context for faculty work. These models and others (Toombs, 1975) initiated a major paradigm shift to a more multifaceted view of faculty development. But while Gaff observed that the most successful programs needed to include elements of all three approaches in some kind of comprehensive plan, the agenda of many programs in the Age of the Teacher placed a primary emphasis on the improvement of teaching through whatever institutional strengths and resources—staffing, budget, programs—were available. Improving teaching was perhaps perceived as an easier starting point than changing an institutional environment.

While individual consultations, workshops, and grants remained key services during the Age of the Developer, some teaching and learning centers or programs also began to bring groups of faculty together to work on achieving common goals for instructional development and curricular change within and across disciplines. A specific faculty development program that was highly successful in creating and sustaining intensive, collaborative teaching and learning forums was the Lilly Teaching Fellows Program, sponsored by the Lilly Endowment. This program encouraged cohorts of early career faculty in research-intensive institutions to work together and with mentors over an academic year to share ideas on teaching and offer one another collegial support, a model sustained to this day (Austin, 1992; Cox, 1995; Cox & Richlin, 2004; Simpson & Jackson, 1990; Sorcinelli & Austin, 1992).

Another impetus for collaborative ventures was the series of academic challenges that arose around the curriculum—challenges that could not be addressed by individual faculty members. These included improving general education, strengthening and assessing academic majors, attending to issues of gender, race, and class, and enhancing learning skills, such as writing and critical thinking, across the curriculum (Gaff & Simpson, 1994). Indeed, teaching and learning communities like the Lilly Teaching Fellowship were expanded throughout the 1980s and 1990s to tackle issues such as diversity, technology, assessment, and general education (Cox, 2001; Ouellett & Sorcinelli, 1995; Shih & Sorcinelli, 2000). Writing across the curriculum, course development, and curricular change projects were highlighted in the Bush Foundation study as particularly effective, not only in terms of helping faculty to develop particular skills such as establishing course goals and teaching writing, but also in facilitating interaction and cooperation across disciplinary boundaries (Eble & McKeachie, 1985). As Gaff and Simpson (1994) concluded, "For each of these agendas, faculty development became the means to the end of curriculum change . . . . Faculty development for curriculum change required groups of faculty to work together to see their own individual interest within the context of the department or institution" (p. 170).

The 1990s pressed both instructors and faculty developers to learn an incredible range of new skills for facilitating teaching and student learning, thus expanding the demands on a number of teaching and learning centers. Perhaps the fastest-moving change in the Age of the Learner was in instructional technology. Faculty moved from using overheads and VCRs to using PowerPoint, streaming video, web-based course management systems such as WebCT and Blackboard, and distance-learning systems. Centers were increasingly called upon to support these instructional tools through teaching technology staff and services (Zhu & Kaplan, 2002).

Scholarly research began to document the value of student diversity to individual students, institutions, and society (Hurtado, 1996; Regents of the University of Michigan 1997–2005) and, in response, some teaching and learning centers made considerable efforts to infuse diversity awareness into their orientations, workshops, publications, and other teaching development activities (Cook & Sorcinelli, 1999). Furthermore, as the value of learner-centered teaching (Barr & Tagg, 1995) was increasingly emphasized, faculty developers played a key role in supporting faculty efforts to explore the effective use of "traditional" active-learning activities such reading, writing, and listening, as well as newer cooperative, collaborative, problem-based, and inquiry-based learning strategies (McKeachie, 2002).

Interest in the assessment of student learning filtered down from institutional approaches in the 1980s (Ewell, 1985) to classroom and course-based assessment in the 1990s (Angelo & Cross, 1993; Walvoord & Anderson, 1998). Here again, teaching and learning centers were instrumental in helping faculty systematically collect and analyze information to assess student learning and their teaching. The boundaries between teaching development and evaluation became more fluid, with collaborations among centers for teaching and learning and offices of assessment more common (Stassen & Sorcinelli, 2001).

In a related vein, Ernest Boyer's book *Scholarship Reconsidered* (1990) stimulated discussion throughout higher education about the nature of scholarship. Boyer and his colleague, Gene Rice, suggested that teachers who devise better ways to help students learn, or who do research on teaching and student learning, are engaged in scholarly work. The outgrowth of this notion was a Scholarship of Teaching and Learning (SOTL) movement initiated through the Carnegie Foundation for the Advancement of Teaching and AAHE. Now, a national network of institutions participate in SOTL. It has engaged colleges, universities, and teaching and learning centers in supporting classroom research, peer review of teaching, the use of course and teaching portfolios, and publications presenting the scholarship of teaching and learning (Hutchings, 2000).

Finally, the continued need to support faculty across the career span was recognized and responded to, both inside and outside of teaching and learning centers. Widespread criticism of the underpreparation of graduate students for teaching careers and broader faculty roles led to new initiatives such as training programs for teaching assistants (Lambert & Tice, 1993), Preparing Future Faculty initiatives (Gaff, Pruitt-Logan, Weibel, & Associates, 2000; Pruitt-Logan & Gaff, 2004), Re-envisioning the Ph.D. (Nyquist, Woodford, & Rogers, 2004), the Carnegie Initiative on the Doctorate (Hutchings & Clarke, 2004), and the Toward the Responsive Ph.D. Initiative (Weisbuch, 2004). In *Paths to the Professoriate*, Wulff and Austin (2004) offer a compendium of recent research and initiatives. In addition, there were more programs and practices to support new and early career faculty, such as new faculty orientations, tenure preparation seminars, and mentoring programs (Rice, Sorcinelli, & Austin, 2000; Sorcinelli, 2000). And while mid-career and senior faculty traditionally received less support than newcomers, some teaching and learning centers created faculty development programs for senior faculty (Cox, 2001; Shih & Sorcinelli, 2000; Stassen & Sorcinelli, 2001) and tenured faculty undergoing post-tenure review (e.g., http://www.umass.edu/cft/teaching_development.htm).

Our review of faculty development program web sites at the cusp of the Age of the Network illuminated the result of these increasing demands on the teaching and learning front. We found that even modest-sized faculty development programs often offer a "cafeteria" of services, and, as a backdrop to our findings, it seems useful to provide a brief review of what services are typically offered. Prior studies of the field have reported a fair degree of consistency in the kinds of resources offered by faculty development programs (Centra, 1976; Erickson, 1986). More recent surveys (Gullatt & Weaver, 1997; Wright, 2002) have continued to find similar services regardless of the size or mission of the institution. These services include:

- *Consultations for individual instructors.* The consultation process may include several phases: clarification of instructional goals; assessment of teaching (e.g., review of course materials, feedback from students, classroom observation, videotaping); analysis of information gathered; establishment of improvement efforts; and review of progress. Consultants often suggest classroom assessment techniques and mid-semester student feedback so that instructors can better understand the learning process and the impact of their teaching on students.

- *University-wide orientations.* Many centers offer orientation programs for new faculty and, separately, for new teaching assistants, both domestic and international. They may include keynote speakers, workshops with tips on "getting started" in teaching, graduate school, and faculty careers. Experienced teaching assistants and faculty often lead training workshops and share their approaches to teaching.

- *University-wide workshops.* Centers and programs also present, on an ongoing basis, a variety of workshops for full-time faculty, teaching assistants, and/or part-time faculty. Subject matter ranges from interactive lecturing to building web pages to infusing multiculturalism into a course and the teaching of it. Workshop leaders vary from in-house and campus facilitators to external experts. Individual academic departments and schools may request customized programs to address instructional questions or problems identified by the unit.

- *Intensive programs.* Some programs offer intensive seminars (from a weeklong institute to yearlong learning communities) for faculty at different career stages or those interested in a particular teaching and learning topic. Signature aspects of yearlong seminars (e.g., the Lilly Teaching Fellowship) include an immersion retreat at the outset, a monthly seminar on teaching and learning, individual consultations, mentoring, and a teaching development project. Other intensive programs include teaching and learning institutes, faculty learning communities, book clubs, special-interest communities, and regular meetings of groups in a breakfast or luncheon format.

- *Grants and awards for individuals and departments.* Programs often offer grant competitions to encourage exploration of new and improved instructional approaches, for conference presentations of successful teaching methods, or for reporting on research findings. Grant amounts range widely depending on available resources. Some programs select faculty associates who receive funding to enrich the activities offered by the center. Programs may also engage in the selection process for campus teaching awards and in the preparation of nominees for external awards such as the Hesburgh Award, the U.S. Professor of the Year Award, or the Robert Foster Cherry Award for Great Teaching.

- *Resources and publications.* Faculty development programs often have a resource room that offers books, videotapes, CD-ROMs, and other instructional materials. Many centers offer on their web sites a range of resources that can be viewed or downloaded, including handbooks, annotated bibliographies, articles, teaching tips, newsletters, and links to other web-based resources.

- *Other services.* Some programs offer specialized services related to instruction, such as student evaluation of teaching instruments, computerized examination and test scoring, programs to assess student learning outcomes, resources in instructional technology, classroom/audio-visual, and distance-learning services.

These are the basic practice models that faculty developers will build upon in the coming years.

Structures

The structured faculty development activities, programs, and policies of the 1950s and 1960s were largely focused on improving scholarly and creative performance. Structures tended to be informal and uncoordinated—an academic chair, dean, or other campus administrator provided the necessary funding for development. At the end of the 1960s, the Project to Improve College Teaching, supported by the American Association of University Professors and ACE, sponsored a series of conferences that included faculty members at some 150 colleges and universities throughout the United States. A key goal of the project was to identify the extent of institutional support for faculty development in teaching. Findings indicated that about 60% of faculty respondents reported specific institutional support for research and only about 10% reported specific support for teaching (Eble, 1972). Thus Eble's study confirmed that faculty development in the Age of the Scholar was focused on research rather than on the improvement of teaching.

A few faculty development units were introduced in the United States during this time. The first was the Center for Research on Learning and Teaching at the University of Michigan, which opened its doors in 1962. The Clinic to Improve University Teaching at the University of Massachusetts Amherst was established soon thereafter. Directors of early units were often outstanding teachers who came out of academic departments (e.g., English, history, psychology) or faculty members with research interests in the teaching and learning process (e.g., psychology, education). These units concentrated primarily on assisting faculty in solving instructional problems or in generating and disseminating research knowledge and information about teaching and learning (Tiberius, 2002).

At the same time that authors and researchers were conceptualizing models for faculty development, campuses were already moving toward practice. Beginning in the 1970s, colleges and universities started to formalize faculty development programs, and centers for teaching and learning began to open on campuses around the country. A series of competitive grant programs for improving teaching fueled their growth (Gaff & Simpson, 1994). Credit is due to private foundations and federally funded agencies, such as the Danforth, W. K. Kellogg, Andrew Mellon, Exxon Education, and National Science Foundations, the Lilly Endowment, the National Endowment for the Humanities, and the Fund for the Improvement of Postsecondary Education, for providing funds for early innovations in teaching and learning.

As the Age of the Developer began, institutional commitment and resources increased, leading to a new emphasis on organizational issues: establishing faculty development priorities, obtaining a wider range of staff expertise, deciding the location of the office—both physically and within the organizational hierarchy—and locating sources of funding (Alstete, 2000). Centers for teaching and learning were often uncoupled from the unit that handled student evaluations of teaching. In fact, many centers developed or confirmed guiding principles that made sure the program was voluntary, confidential, and developmental rather than evaluative, and built a firewall between teaching development work and personnel decision-making processes (Sorcinelli, 2002). At the same time, centers for teaching and learning often collaborated with undergraduate deans, graduate deans, and writing program directors on faculty development initiatives, such as teaching assistant training, or curricular initiatives, such as general education, writing across the curriculum, and freshman seminars.

At the end of the 1980s, faculty developers, as well as faculty and administrators interested in promoting and sustaining faculty development programs in their institutions, were further guided by the POD Network, which developed *A Handbook for New Practitioners* (Wadsworth, 1988). This book served as a fundamental resource for both new and seasoned faculty developers and offered practical information on faculty development topics such as setting up a faculty development program, assessing teaching practices, offering a range of programs and services, and reaching specific audiences. In 2002, Gillespie, Hilsen, and Wadsworth edited a second book, *A Guide to Faculty Development*, to provide more up-to-date advice, examples, and resources for developers and their institutions.

The 1990s saw continued growth in faculty development programs, despite the much publicized closing of a prominent teaching and learning center at a large research university. Critical to the success of many centers was a high-quality staff of instructional developers who may or may not have come from faculty ranks but typically had Ph.D.s in a variety of fields, college teaching experience, and experience working with colleagues on teaching improvements. Some had specialized expertise in instructional technology, evaluation research, course and program assessment, and multicultural education to promote inclusivity. The community of developers in the POD Network became increasingly well connected through their annual meeting, several journals and newsletters, and an active listserv. This network of professionals expanded annually as more new teaching centers were established (Cook & Sorcinelli, 2002). Many centers continued to collaborate with other campus offices (e.g., graduate school, academic computing, library, community service-learning) on institutional priorities, but still relied on institutional funds and private foundations to support their work.

Since their inception, programs for faculty development have shared a common theme: improving the quality of education by working with faculty. There has, however, been considerable variety in program types, depending on institutional leadership, community, faculty, age and historical evolution, and available resources (Wright, 2002). Structural variations among programs occur in how they are organized and where they are located in the institution. The current range of structures includes:

- A *centralized unit* with dedicated staff that is budgeted by the institution to offer a range of faculty development programs. It serves the entire institution, or a substantial segment of it, in a variety of ways.

- An office that serves as a *clearinghouse* for programs and offerings that are sponsored across the institution, but offers few programs itself.

- A *committee* charged with supporting faculty development, usually made up of unpaid volunteer faculty who oversee faculty development offerings.

- *Single individual programs* often run by an administrator responsible for faculty matters or a faculty member with a part-time assignment for development activities.

- *Other programs* such as multicampus, cooperative programs, and special-purpose centers.

Other structural variations can be found in Wright (2002) and at the POD web site (http://www.podnetwork.org). Which type of program will most effectively serve a given institution will remain an important question for developers in the coming years.

Studies

Early appraisals of the effectiveness of faculty development focused primarily on traditional measures of enhanced or renewed scholarly productivity: a completed degree, an increase in scholarly presentations, books, or articles, or the winning of external grants or fellowships. While benefits might accrue to students in terms of their learning or to broader institutional goals such as development of curriculum in the major or student advising, such benefits were assumed rather than measured.

The Project on College Teaching, directed by Kenneth Eble (1972), produced one of the first reports on faculty development efforts. The project reported on career development in college teaching and on the evaluation and recognition of good teaching. Eble concluded that policies and practices in many institutions did not encourage faculty members to improve teaching and argued that paying attention to teaching played a role in institutional vitality and quality. This early study provided a stimulus for interest in faculty development activities to improve teaching and a prototype for reports about the results of grants given for faculty development.

The first large-scale study of faculty development was conducted by Centra in 1976, in a survey to which 756 U.S. colleges and universities responded. His goals were to identify faculty development activities, to evaluate their effectiveness, to determine funding sources, and to identify various organizational structures for faculty development programs. More than 40% of the institutions had a unit or a person that coordinated the faculty or instructional development activities on their campus. The majority of units had one full- or part-time person who served as director or coordinator.

Interestingly, 25% of institutions were part of a consortium or regional group (e.g., Great Lakes Colleges Consortium) that concentrated on faculty development. Cooperative arrangements were found most often in four-year liberal arts colleges, enabling such schools to share expertise and activities at lower cost to each institution.

Perhaps the most valuable aspect of the study was the identification of groups of services and activities that institutions used and considered particularly effective in promoting faculty development. These included traditional practices (e.g., sabbaticals, leaves, summer grants), instructional assistance (e.g., use of teaching consultants to assist individual faculty in developing teaching skills), workshops (e.g., on specific instructional or advising strategies), grants and travel funds, and assessment techniques (e.g., ratings of instruction by students). In terms of measuring the outcomes of faculty development programs, Centra found that only 14% of faculty development programs were evaluated, with an additional 33% reporting some partial evaluation. Suggested reasons for not documenting faculty development outcomes included limitations in staff, funding, and knowledge of assessment practices (Centra, 1976).

The 1970s also provided a closer look at faculty development in community colleges and liberal arts colleges. At community colleges, faculty renewal programs looked much like the required, in-service training conducted by public school systems (Lewis, 1998). A 1970 survey by the American Association of Junior Colleges indicated that most faculty development programs involved workshops and short courses on education, curriculum, and learning theories (O'Banion, 1972).

The 1970s concluded with the first evaluation of faculty development programs at undergraduate liberal arts institutions, funded by the Association of American Colleges and the Andrew Mellon Foundation (Nelsen & Siegel, 1980). The project directors visited 20 colleges, and interviewers engaged more than 500 faculty, administrators, and students about a wide range of faculty development activities and their impact. The results of the evaluation suggested that the most frequent and successful activities, as viewed by liberal arts college participants, involved individual professional development options such as study leaves and support for attendance at professional meetings. Projects that focused on discussions and innovations in the curriculum were also viewed quite favorably. Instructional development efforts, especially workshops, were greeted with less enthusiasm unless they were organized to provide specific, usable skills (e.g., lecturing skills, grading practices). Organizational development, with its focus on the institutional environment that creates the context for faculty work, was found to be the most neglected area of faculty development. Interestingly, effective management was identified as the tie that binds the most successful faculty development programs. Important components included the presence of a unit—a committee or group of administrators—with a clear charge and structure, some linkage of faculty development activities to the reward structure of the college, and flexibility in terms of supporting various approaches to faculty development.

The field of faculty development "spawn[ed] a literature throughout the 1970s rich in diagnoses and prescriptions" (Schuster, Wheeler, & Associates, 1990, p. 3), but it was not until the 1980s that the literature was enriched with more evidence of the systematic evaluation of programs. In 1986, Erickson, on behalf of the POD Network, conducted a survey of faculty development practices, adapted from Centra's (1976) survey a decade earlier. Erickson received responses from some 630 faculty development coordinators, directors, committee chairs, and administrators. He found that "50% or more of our four-year colleges, universities and professional schools offer some formal faculty development, instructional development, or teaching improvement services" (p. 196), up from about 40% a decade earlier. A committee or an administrator—typically a dean whose primary responsibilities lay elsewhere—most often coordinated these activities. While documenting a steady growth in faculty development services, Erickson noted that only 14% of institutions had dedicated centers and another 14% had coordinators or directors of faculty development.

The survey also assessed availability of the following services: workshops and seminars; assessment practices; individual consultation; grants, leaves, and exchanges; and other practices. Erickson (1986), similar to Centra (1976), found that "traditional" practices like grants, awards, leaves, and exchanges were the most frequently offered services. Individual consultation services were available at the fewest numbers of institutions. Not surprisingly, larger institutions offered a greater variety of services than smaller ones. He also discovered that 95% of the campuses made available student ratings of instruction, although less than half provided faculty with individual help from consultants trained to interpret such ratings.

During this decade, there were several other key scholarly studies that either evaluated faculty development programs or investigated the connections among faculty development, faculty career stages, and institutional missions. For example, Baldwin and Blackburn (1981) researched the distinguishing characteristics of faculty members at successive ages and in different career stages and advocated mapping faculty development activities with career stages. Clark, Corcoran, and Lewis's (1986) study of faculty vitality proposed an approach to faculty development that emphasized linking faculty work to institutional missions and needs.

Eble and McKeachie (1985) analyzed a wide variety of faculty development programs in 24 different institutions—public and private, small liberal arts colleges to research universities—supported by the Bush Foundation. Their overall message was positive. They found that while traditional practices such as leaves and grants were still valued by faculty, instructional development activities and projects involving course development and curricular change were both popular and highly effective. They also argued that faculty development programs "were rallying points for renewed interest in teaching during a time of considerable need at virtually all of the participating institutions" (p. 158) and could make a difference in faculty vitality. Finally, they identified key factors influencing faculty development program success, including faculty ownership, administrative support, use of local expertise, sustained or follow-up activities, and programs involving faculty members working together to achieve common objectives.

Two works reviewed the literature on faculty development, providing easily accessible sources of information for researchers and practitioners. Bland and Schmitz (1988) conducted a systematic analysis of faculty development literature from 1965 to 1985. They concluded that the literature base had grown considerably in the early 1980s, suggesting increased interest in the field. They also found that strategies and recommendations for faculty development had become more multidimensional—drawn from individual, departmental, and institutional perspectives. Menges and Mathis (1988) developed a comprehensive guide to more than 600 books and articles on teaching, learning, curriculum, and faculty development in colleges and universities. The authors offered a critical evaluation of the most significant theory and research on these four essential topics and illuminated the role each has had in shaping and advancing theory and practice in higher education.

Alstete (2000) conducted a search of faculty development literature from 1989–1997, which showed an initial increase in the early 1990s and a slightly upward trend in the amount of faculty development literature as the decade progressed. He concluded that while interest in and descriptive literature about how institutions have engaged in effective faculty development programs have grown, there is more work to be done to build and articulate "a clearly defined supporting theory underlying faculty development" (p. 28).

During the 1990s, there were no large-scale studies of the field to follow up the research of Centra (1976) and Erickson (1986). There were, however, a number of studies and reviews that explored various aspects of faculty development practices. Hellyer and Boschmann (1993) reviewed information on faculty development programs gathered from 94 institutions of higher education, drawn in part from a description of programs compiled by members of the POD Network. Their goal was to identify common practices. As in earlier studies, the authors found great variance in the depth and breadth of programs. The authors reported that for the most part the creation of faculty development centers had been relatively recent. While one program began in the 1940s and a few in the 1960s, 50% of the institutions surveyed started their programs in the 1980s. By far the most common faculty development practices were workshops and discussions (93%). Other activities included individual consultations (63%), new faculty orientations and teaching assistant training (60%), research on teaching (51%), and teaching grants (34%). The authors concluded from the materials they surveyed that faculty strongly support the existence of faculty development offices.

Wright and O'Neil (1995) surveyed an international community of faculty developers in Canada, the United States, the United Kingdom, and Australasia. Data from 331 respondents suggested "what works" within the wide range of practices for the support of teaching and learning. Findings pointed to the critical role of academic deans and department chairs, of employment practices that recognize and reward good teaching, and of institutionalized teaching centers that offer development opportunities such as mentoring programs for new teachers, grants, and workshops.

Crawley (1995) surveyed 104 research universities to learn about faculty development programs available to senior faculty. The findings revealed a high level of support for traditional approaches to faculty development (e.g., sabbaticals, unpaid leaves, grants), but suggested that faculty development approaches that expanded employment options or created new roles and responsibilities for senior faculty were more limited.

Chism and Szabo (1996) surveyed a random sample of 100 institutions drawn from the POD Network to determine who used faculty development services. In part, the study was a response to the common perception that "good" teachers use faculty development services, while "bad" teachers eschew them (Angelo & Cross, 1993; Boice, 1984; Centra, 1976). Again, because faculty development programs varied so greatly in mission, composition of potential clients, and range of services offered, it was difficult for the authors to aggregate data and provide simple answers on the extent of faculty use. They found, however, that most faculty development programs kept records on who used what services. For the 70% of programs with data on usage, the survey determined that the average program reached 82% of users through publications, 47% through events, 11% through consultation, and 8% through mentoring programs. Overall, use of services was fairly distributed across faculty ranks, with assistant professors accounting for a somewhat higher percentage of use. Females used faculty development services at somewhat higher rates than males, and only slight differences among the disciplines were reported. The authors also found "some support for the claim that faculty are motivated both by interest in teaching and by difficulties" (p. 120). Murray (2002) reviewed faculty development literature and practices in community colleges, turning up few national or regional studies and finding some serious methodological questions in many of the single-institution studies. Still, some consistent themes emerged from the literature. In many community colleges, faculty development programs lacked goals—especially goals tied to the college's mission. Few programs attempted to evaluate their work, and faculty participation was low. Successful programs tended to have conditions that mirrored the results of earlier researchers and practitioners (Eble & McKeachie, 1985; Sorcinelli, 2002): administrative support that encourages faculty development; a formal, structured, goal-directed program; connections between faculty development and the reward structure; faculty ownership; and collegial support for investment in teaching. These principles of good practice in faculty development seem to have held true across a range of institutions and throughout the decades.

Most recently, in addition to the study that forms the basis of this book, two electronic surveys of POD Network members have been conducted. One surveyed 27 previous presidents of the POD Network and opinion leaders in higher education (Sell, 2002) and the other surveyed 109 directors of teaching and learning centers (Frantz, Beebe, Horvath, Canales, & Swee, 2005). Key themes in these studies include accountability practices of faculty development centers, best practices, resources and services provided by teaching and learning centers, and future strategies for faculty development.

Conclusion

The history of faculty development, then, is one of both challenge and opportunity. Since its inception, faculty development has proven its capacity to anticipate and respond to changes and to act as a lever of change in higher education. It has evolved from individual to collective development, from singular to multidimensional purposes, from largely uncoordinated activities to centralized units, from "soft" funding to foundation, association, government, and institutional support, and from a small network of developers in the United States to a global faculty development profession. Its measurable impact has increased along with these changes.

We believe that in the Age of the Network the changes facing institutions will continue to accelerate. Colleges and universities committed to high productivity and quality will be well advised to situate faculty development at the center of their institutional planning. The future of faculty development may depend on our collective ability to fashion guiding principles and practices for the field that acknowledge new responsibilities while sustaining core values, and to articulate their significance to higher education. The next three chapters illustrate some of the opportunities and challenges currently engaging faculty developers, faculty members, and their institutions. What goals and practices will best serve faculty developers in the coming years is the subject of last three chapters of this book.

Chapter highlights

- In the Age of the Scholar (1950s and early 1960s) the term *faculty development* referred primarily to practices for improving scholarly competence. Few colleges and universities had formal programs and there were few studies of faculty development efforts.

- In the Age of the Teacher (mid 1960s through 1970s), the field expanded to include faculty, instructional, and organizational development, but primarily focused attention on improving teaching. Foundation support spurred campuses to create faculty development programs. Faculty development secured a professional identity through the founding of two associations in the United States.

- In the Age of the Developer (1980s), faculty development broadened to address curricular issues, faculty needs at different career stages, and collective as well as individual faculty growth. Programs were increasingly supported by institutional and external funds, creating heightened interest in measuring the outcomes of teaching and faculty development efforts. Canada created its own society for teaching, learning, and faculty development.

- In the Age of the Learner (1990s) the number of teaching and learning centers continued to increase; the number of issues, their level of complexity, and the scope of activities expanded. Multiple venues for faculty development proposals and recognition were created within educational associations, foundations, professional societies, and international consortia.

- In the current Age of the Network, faculty development programs continue to grow in breadth and use. Developers will be called upon to preserve, clarify, and enhance the purposes of faculty development, and to network with faculty and institutional leaders to respond to institutional problems and propose constructive solutions as we meet the challenges of the new century.

2

A Portrait of Current Faculty Development: Personnel and Programs

To consider the future of faculty development, we began by reviewing its history, and then conducted a survey to collect the views of faculty developers today. (See Appendix 1 for the complete survey.) "Envisioning the Future of Faculty Development: A Survey of Faculty Development Professionals" explored the demographics of current faculty developers, including titles and length of time respondents have held positions in faculty development and the structures of their institutions' faculty development programs. Developers were queried about the goals and purposes of current faculty development programs, influences on current faculty development programs and practice, and services currently offered and the importance of those services. Next, developers were asked to identify the top challenges facing faculty members, institutions, and faculty development programs. The survey also asked faculty developers about their views concerning potential new directions for the field. Finally, we provided open-ended questions to which developers could respond by sharing their concerns, ideas, and advice for improving future faculty development practices. The comments collected in the surveys reflected a vast range of experience in and knowledge of faculty development, issues facing higher education, and current research regarding teaching and learning.

The Study Design

A few issues concerning the survey and the respondents require special note. The population we studied were members of the Professional and Organizational Development Network in Higher Education (POD Network), the oldest and largest professional association of faculty development scholars and practitioners in higher education. The survey was sent to the full POD Network mailing list for 2001 (999 names). We received completed surveys from 494 people at 300 institutions in the United States and 31 institutions in Canada, for an overall response rate of 50%, slightly higher than the response rate to an earlier survey of POD Network membership (Graf & Wheeler, 1996). The response rate from Canadian POD Network members was 53% and from U.S. members, 49%. Thirty-nine percent of the respondents were men and 61% were women.

We asked respondents to indicate their institution's type according to the 1994 Carnegie classification system. We opted to use this long-established system for identification purposes since the application of the new 2000 Carnegie classification scheme was not universal when we conducted and analyzed our survey. Table 2.1 shows the percentages of respondents from each institutional type. The largest cohort of respondents (44%) work at research or doctoral institutions. Because the number of respondents from doctoral institutions was relatively small (38), and their responses differed little from those at research institutions, we collapsed those categories. Almost another quarter (23%) work at comprehensive universities. The remaining group is distributed among liberal arts colleges (11%), community colleges (9%), and Canadian colleges and universities (8%). The "other" category (5%) includes those who work at medical and professional schools, state systems of institutions, tribal colleges, and proprietary schools. In reporting findings, there are instances where the U.S. and Canadian data are reported separately, primarily when we present data based on institutional types. Canadian institutions are not listed in the Carnegie Classification system.

The POD Network has many members from large universities, which tend to have well-established faculty development programs. Therefore the proportion of respondents from research and doctoral universities (44%) exceeds the representation of such institutions nationally (7%). The same pattern holds, though to a lesser extent, for respondents from comprehensive institutions. The proportion of respondents from liberal arts colleges (11%) was a bit less than the proportion of such institutions nationally (15%). Only 9% of respondents were from community colleges, underrepresenting the percentage of community colleges among all institutional types (42%). Many community college developers may choose to belong to the National Council for Staff, Program, and Organizational Development (NCSPOD), an organization for community college faculty developers. The American Association of Community Colleges recognized NCSPOD as one of its affiliate councils in 1978.

Table 2.1: Respondents by Institutional Type, 1994 Carnegie Classification

Carnegie Classification	Respondents	Percent
Research and Doctoral	206	44%
Comprehensive I and II	110	23%
Liberal Arts I and II	51	11%
Community College	42	9%
Other	23	5%
Canadian	39	8%

N = 471; Unreported = 23

We recognize that this census of faculty developers, while representative of the membership of the field's largest professional organization, may not represent the scope and proportion of all faculty development professionals and programs across the U.S. and Canada.

Titles of Respondents

We asked respondents to indicate all the titles they hold at their institutions, as well as the title they consider primary (see Table 2.2). One-third of the respondents (33%) listed their primary title as director of faculty development. Almost one-quarter identified their faculty role as primary (21%) and a similar percentage (23%) identified themselves as senior administrators (e.g., associate provost, associate vice chancellor) or midlevel administrators (e.g., academic dean, associate dean, department chair). Seventy percent of the respondents reported holding two titles. The most prevalent combinations of titles were "director" or "associate/assistant director" and "faculty member," with 60% of respondents indicating that they were a director of a center also holding a faculty appointment. Thus it is not unusual for individuals responsible for faculty development at their institutions to hold more than one position. Those with faculty status as well as an administrative title may be perceived as more credible on issues of teaching and learning because of their direct involvement in the classroom.

Table 2.2: Primary Titles of Respondents

Title	Respondents	Percent
Director	153	33%
Program Coordinator	34	7%
Senior-Level Administrator	63	14%
Midlevel Administrator	40	9%
Faculty Member	99	21%
Assistant/Associate Director	41	9%
Technology Coordinator	5	1%
Instructional Development Consultant	21	5%
Other	4	1%

N = 460; Unreported = 34

Although the primary title of respondents varied by institutional type, as indicated in Table 2.3, more than two-thirds of the respondents indicated a primary title that was administrative in nature, with the exception of developers in community colleges, where the highest percentage of responses came from individuals who identified themselves primarily as faculty members (37%).

Table 2.3: Primary Titles of Respondents by Institutional Type

Title	R/D	Comp	LA	CC	Can	Other
Director	34%	39%	24%	21%	44%	33%
Assistant /Associate Director	14%	1%	6%	3%	15%	10%
Senior-Level Administrator	16%	14%	16%	11%	5%	19%
Midlevel Administrator	7%	8%	22%	13%	0%	5%
Coordinator	18%	7%	4%	15%	21%	9%
Faculty Member	11%	31%	28%	37%	15%	24%

N = 438; Unreported = 23; R/D = Research/Doctoral; Comp = Comprehensive;
LA = Liberal Arts; CC = Community College; Can = Canadian

New and Experienced Developers

A goal of the survey was to discover how long respondents had held a position of responsibility in faculty development. Although faculty development programs were introduced in the 1960s, this study suggests that current faculty development professionals are fairly new to the field. In reviewing the data, we categorized "new developers" as individuals with five or fewer years of experience, and "experienced developers" as those with more than ten years of experience. Overall, more than half of the respondents clustered in the new developers category. Only about a quarter fell into the category of experienced developers. In terms of institutional type, community college developers reported the highest average number of years of experience, while those at comprehensive universities reported the lowest average.

We then looked at respondents' number of years in faculty development, organized according to their primary title and responsibility (see Table 2.4). Among directors of faculty development programs, a surprisingly large group (43%) had five or fewer years of faculty development experience. Thus a large percentage of respondents who are relatively new to faculty development hold the title of director. Likewise, well over half of associate and assistant directors, program coordinators, midlevel administrators, and faculty members also had five or fewer years of experience. The majority of respondents with more than 10 years of experience were in positions other than director of faculty development. Only about one-third of directors had more than 10 years of experience; the same was true for senior-level administrators responsible for guiding faculty development efforts.

Table 2.4: Average Years in Faculty Development by Primary Title

Title	< = 5 years	6–10 years	11–14 years	> = 15 years
Director	43%	24%	9%	24%
Program Coordinator	66%	16%	9%	9%
Senior-Level Administrator	37%	32%	8%	23%
Midlevel Administrator	72%	18%	10%	0%
Faculty Member	61%	19%	7%	13%
Assistant/Associate Director	56%	20%	17%	7%
Technology Coordinator	60%	40%	0%	0%
Instructional Development Consultant	38%	24%	5%	33%
Other	75%	0%	25%	0%

The amount of experience developers reported supports an image of faculty development on the move. The high percentage of inexperienced developers indicates the recent extensive growth of faculty development programs across the country. This pattern holds even for developers in leadership positions (e.g., directors and associate directors). The profession seems to be aware of the need to make skills training and professional orientation available for the new developer. For example, the POD Network offers a day-long workshop prior to its annual conference, a summer institute, and print resources in which experienced developers guide newcomers in setting up and sustaining faculty development centers (Gillespie, Hilsen, & Wadsworth, 2002). NCSPOD and the Institute for Community College Development offer a yearlong training program in staff, program, and organizational development. Upon completion, developers receive a certificate recognizing their achievement. For more information see http://www.ncspod.org/spod.php.

While a large number of developers are new to the field, it is important to note that 24% of respondents whose primary title is "director" and 23% of those whose primary title is "senior-level administrator" have been involved in faculty development for 15 or more years. Among those who indicated "instructional development coordinator," one-third have more than 15 years in faculty development. Thus novices can draw advice from a small cadre of seasoned colleagues. Recently, some center directors have moved into positions such as associate provost, vice chancellor, and advisor to the president. These titles suggest the legitimization of faculty development as central to the mission of institutions.

Technology is one of the most compelling issues in higher education overall and in faculty development in particular. Respondents are deeply concerned about and engaged in issues of technology and teaching, yet only a small fraction (1%) of the survey respondents identified their primary title as "technology coordinator." It may be that technology coordinators involved in faculty development are largely affiliated with organizations other than the POD Network, or are located in information technology or other technology-oriented campus departments and thus were not captured as part of this survey. The small percentage of faculty developers who identified themselves as technology coordinators raises the question of whether—and how—faculty development programs are incorporating technological issues into their concerns about teaching and learning. Not surprisingly, the technology coordinators who did respond to the survey are the newest in the field of faculty development—none reported more than 10 years of experience.

In summary, the data suggest that individuals responsible for faculty development in the 21st century hold multiple titles and have multiple responsibilities to go along with them. The majority of respondents identify themselves as administrators (e.g., directors, associate directors, coordinators), and three-fifths of all developers hold faculty appointments as well. Perhaps most striking, as a group they tend to be relatively new to the field, with only one-quarter reporting that they have been in faculty development for a decade or more.

Structures of Faculty Development

The purpose of the next section of the survey was to determine how institutions currently structure their faculty development programs. To better understand how faculty development efforts are currently structured within institutions and how those structures have evolved or changed over time, we asked developers what best described the structure of faculty development efforts at their institution: a centralized unit with dedicated staff that offers a range of faculty development programs; a clearinghouse for programs and offerings sponsored across the institution that offers few programs itself; a committee charged with supporting faculty development; an individual faculty member or administrator charged with supporting faculty development; or another type of arrangement not listed. We modeled the descriptions we offered respondents on earlier research and literature (Centra, 1976; Erickson, 1986; Wright, 2002) and our experiences with different faculty development structures.

Because results pertaining to faculty development structures and program goals were sometimes skewed by multiple responses within the same U.S. institution, we used a single response in these cases, that of the respondent with the most senior position. Faculty development structures of the 300 institutions represented in the survey can be categorized as follows:

- A centralized unit with dedicated staff (54%)
- Individual faculty member or administrator (19%)
- A committee that supports faculty development (12%)
- A clearinghouse for programs and offerings (4%)
- Other structures, such as system-wide offices or combinations (11%)

A study published in the mid 1980s found that the most common structure for faculty development was that of an individual dean or administrator charged with responsibility for faculty development among other duties (Erickson, 1986). Only 14% of the institutions Erickson surveyed had dedicated faculty development centers or programs. Another 14% had coordinators or directors of faculty development, and yet another 14% had committees that coordinated services (as opposed to 62% of committees that served in an advisory role).

Our findings, presented in Table 2.5, demonstrate a dramatic increase during the past 15 years across all institutions in the number of centralized units with dedicated staff (54%). This trend is particularly evident among research and doctoral institutions (72%). Overall, these figures suggest a shift in patterns. The organizational structure for faculty development is now more often one in which programming is coordinated by an identifiable, centralized unit with professional staff and less often one in which activities are anchored to a single midlevel administrator with other responsibilities or to an advisory committee.

Cook and Sorcinelli (2002) suggest why many more institutions have chosen to establish centralized teaching centers. At their best, these centers serve as respected symbols of an institution's commitment to the teaching mission

and educational quality. They have the institutional memory to provide con-
tinuity in teaching support services throughout transitions of department
chairs, deans, and provosts. They gather professionals with special expertise in
teaching and learning issues and provide a location for sponsoring and high-
lighting instructional innovations, and they offer confidentiality for individual instructors seeking either to improve their teaching practice or to explore
new avenues for enhancing student learning. By facilitating networking
among faculty and administrators across the campus, developers often serve
as change agents to help institutions deepen their teaching missions.

Faculty development structures tallied from the most senior developer at
each surveyed institution in Canadian universities evidenced a similar pattern. There was a strong preference for centralized units with dedicated staff
(71%). Another 16% were led by an individual faculty member or administrator, 8% were coordinated by a committee, and 3% offered a clearinghouse
for campus-wide programs. Canadian scholars such as Donald (1997) have
urged universities to establish teaching and learning centers, suggesting that
they can serve as resource centers and introduce new developments in post-
secondary education to the university. Our findings indicate that there has
been a positive response to such recommendations.

Table 2.5: Faculty Development Structure by Institutional Type—U.S. Responses

	All	**R/D**	**Comp**	**LA**	**CC**	**Other**
Central Unit	54%	72%	51%	24%	34%	50%
Clearinghouse	4%	5%	2%	0%	17%	0%
Committee	12%	3%	12%	26%	21%	12%
Individual	19%	10%	24%	33%	21%	19%
Other	11%	10%	11%	17%	7%	19%
(generally combination)						

N = 285; Unreported = 15; R/D = Research/Doctoral; Comp = Comprehensive;
LA = Liberal Arts; CC = Community College

Institutional differences

Although the trend across campuses has been toward institutionalization of faculty development programs, faculty development models and structures remain strongly related to institutional type. For example, research and doctoral universities generally organize their faculty development programs as campus-wide centers that serve the entire institution, or a substantial segment of it, in a variety of ways. According to Wright (2002), the typical campus-wide center is organized administratively under the chief academic officer, usually the provost. Leadership may be selected from the faculty; however, there is a growing pool of experienced faculty developers who assume leadership roles in such centers. Staff members in campus-wide centers often include a director, an associate or assistant director, one or two faculty developers, part-time graduate assistants, and a secretary. Centers are often supported by the institution's base budget, sometimes supplemented by grant funds for special projects, and they usually serve faculty at all stages of their careers—from graduate teaching assistants to senior faculty. See Wright (2002) for detailed descriptions of services offered and examples of various campus-wide centers.

While over half (51%) of the respondents from comprehensive universities also report the presence of central units, about a quarter (24%) organize faculty development initiatives under the direction of an individual faculty member or administrator. Faculty development structures at these institutions include a significant number of single, campus-wide centers with dedicated staff. At the same time, the model of an experienced faculty member or dean who is charged with supporting faculty development remains a viable one at a number of comprehensive university campuses.

Structurally, Wright (2002) describes the model of an individual who is charged with supporting faculty development as "a development component of other academic programs" (p. 32). Most programs of this type are located under a unit such as a dean's office or a faculty development committee. A faculty member with release time may serve as a faculty development consultant, or an administrator may take on this assignment as part of his or her workload. Budgets depend upon unit priorities, and resources may limit the scope of activities offered. Program development is usually the responsibility of a faculty committee made up of unpaid, volunteer faculty who oversee faculty development offerings.

In 1976, Centra found that many small liberal arts colleges, in comparison to larger institutions, were less able or inclined to support either a center or a person with expertise in instructional development. Today, more than half of the liberal arts colleges represented in our survey have either a faculty member or administrator in charge of faculty development (33%) or a central unit (24%). Further evidence of the growth of development programs in the liberal arts colleges can be seen in the establishment of a Small Colleges Committee by the POD Network, founded by the director of a teaching and learning center at a small liberal arts college. Its goal is to coordinate the interests of persons working in small college settings.

While the number of campus-wide centers is expanding at liberal arts colleges, the use of teachers or other expert faculty members to help colleagues clearly remains a structural part of faculty development. Individuals with faculty status who take the lead in teaching and learning initiatives are likely to have established respect and stature in the institution. The comments from one center's director capture the challenging context in which some faculty developers operate at liberal arts colleges: "I am the only professional (with less than half-time clerical support) for a teaching and learning center that was created two years ago. Most of my time has been spent addressing the development of student support programs. While there is a huge need for faculty development, I have had very little time to give to it."

Liberal arts institutions reported the greatest use of committees charged with supporting faculty development (26%). In these schools a faculty development committee may be directed or coordinated by a dean, associate dean, or faculty member. The committee may have its own budget to support travel, mentoring and orientation programs, workshops, and other activities. Faculty development at small colleges may also focus on a particular aspect of faculty and/or student development, such as technology, writing, speaking, or student achievement. It should be noted that the faculty development committee may exist along with a faculty development center. Lunde and Healy (2002) present a particularly useful guide for establishing a faculty development committee and answer questions about the nature, goals, structures, and activities of such committees.

The faculty development structures within community colleges evidenced the most variation. Over a third of the institutions represented have central units (34%), while the other two-thirds have nearly equal numbers of programs that center on an individual (21%), committee (21%), or clearinghouse (17%). The clearinghouse model is used to a much greater degree by community colleges than by any other institutional type. Typically, a single individual provides a repository for faculty development resources and coordinates efforts across units. On a larger scale, this model has also been used in "multi-campus cooperative programs" (Wright, 2002, p. 30). Such programs usually have a central office that coordinates efforts and administers resources for a number of institutions. Either the single individual or central office variation can offer opportunities for intra- and inter-institutional communication.

Many factors contribute to the range of structural variations in faculty development programs in community colleges. As noted in Chapter 1, research on faculty development has highlighted the need for community colleges to match more closely faculty development goals with institutional mission (Murray, 2002). Academic leaders in these colleges may require more structural variation in order to fit local culture and deliver faculty development programming that best meets institutional priorities.

Goals Guiding Faculty Development Programs

Our study is the first to specifically ask developers what goals guide their programs. Of course, the overarching goal for all faculty development programs is to improve student learning. Our operating assumption is that the positive actions of individual faculty and the collective impact of faculty development programs are beneficial to that process, and we are especially interested in what developers have identified as the primary goals that carried them toward the ultimate goal of facilitating learning for their institutions' students.

Successful faculty development programs articulate their guiding principles and essential goals (Sorcinelli, 2002). Such a statement need not be elaborate, but it does need to be formulated clearly and communicated regularly to the institution (e.g., through an annual report, a program brochure, or a unit plan). This conceptual framework can also help in outlining core activities, guiding budgetary decisions, and prioritizing the use of limited resources.

Developers read 10 statements of goals and purposes (based on our experience and a review of the literature) and ranked them on a 4-point Likert-type scale (1 = Not at All; 2 = To a Slight Extent; 3 = To a Moderate Extent; 4 = To a Great Extent; NS = Not Sure) based on the degree to which the goals guide their programs. Goals listed on the survey included:

- To respond to and support individual faculty members' goals for professional development
- To foster collegiality within and among faculty members and/or departments
- To provide recognition and reward for excellence in teaching
- To create or sustain a culture of teaching excellence
- To advance new initiatives in teaching and learning
- To act as a change agent within the institution
- To respond to critical needs as defined by the institution
- To provide support for faculty members who are experiencing difficulties with their teaching
- To support departmental goals, planning, and development
- To position the institution at the forefront of educational innovation

Respondents were also given the opportunity to add goals and purposes guiding their programs that were not listed. Respondents were then asked to list the three primary goals that guide their programs. We first looked at responses from the senior participant at each institution (N=300), assuming that that person would be most informed about the goals guiding faculty development at his or her institution. We also compared responses from the other developers who responded to the survey and found that developers at the same institution—from junior to senior—did not differ significantly in their choice of key goals.

Primary Goals

Across all U.S. institutional types, the senior faculty developers perceived the top three goals guiding their programs as the following (percentages indicate the portion of the respondents who chose the goal as one of the three primary goals for their programs, as indicated in Table 2.6):

- Creating or sustaining a culture of teaching excellence (72%)
- Responding to individual faculty members' needs (56%)
- Advancing new initiatives in teaching and learning (49%)

These goals reflect the long-standing interest of faculty development programs in advancing teaching and learning issues and in strategies to support individual faculty members. Yet they also reflect a dramatic recognition of the proactive organizational role that faculty development can play in creating an institutional environment supportive of teaching and learning. The comments of a senior administrator at a liberal arts college emphasize the organizational role increasingly expected of faculty development programs: "If we wish to continue to attract and retain excellent faculty we must focus on organizational and faculty development that will foster the intrinsic rewards of a faculty post."

Reaching the primary goal of creating a culture of teaching excellence is not a simple matter; it requires multidimensional strategies and the partnership of administrators, faculty, and faculty developers. Findings from an international study of teaching improvement practices (Wright & O'Neil, 1995), interviews with academic leaders at four premier research universities (Donald, 1997), and a case study of administrative and faculty development collaboration (Sorcinelli & Aitken, 1995) suggest that creating an institutional culture that values teaching requires the support of academic administrators (particularly chairs and deans) and faculty, the recognition of teaching as an important factor in personnel decision-making, the availability of a variety of faculty development opportunities, and the establishment of an institutional unit to promote effective teaching and learning.

Our findings suggest that "responding to individual faculty members' needs and interests" (56%) remains central to the work of faculty developers. Many faculty development programs present a wide variety of approaches for the benefit of faculty members. These may include faculty grants to devise new approaches to teaching, funds for travel to conferences, release time for improving teaching, workshops, semester- or year-long faculty learning communities, individual and departmental consultations, teaching award programs, and print, media, or other technology-based resources (Gillespie, Hilsen, & Wadsworth, 2002).

Interestingly, results of the Centra (1976) and Erickson (1986) studies suggest that in previous decades there was a more singular focus on individual faculty needs and activities than developers in our current study seem to embrace. The percentages of developers who cited the broad goals of "creating or sustaining a culture of teaching excellence" (72%) and "advancing new initiatives in teaching and learning" (49%) indicate the vision of leadership and organizational development that influences faculty developers today. The thoughts of a center director at a research university reflect a shift from an earlier emphasis on the individual growth of teachers to a more inclusive emphasis on student development, community, and institutional culture: "I do think we are more focused on student learning outcomes and teaching that encourages it. I also think faculty development has moved from individual to communal growth in teaching and learning."

Parker Palmer (1998) has called on teachers, administrators, and educational institutions to commit to creating collegial organizational environments that value exploration, renewal, and change. It is satisfying to find that over one-quarter of the respondents (26%) included "fostering collegiality" as one of the three primary goals that guide their programs. Studies confirm that faculty members need one another's support and that many faculty members express the desire to work with colleagues within and outside of their disciplines. In fact, getting to know other faculty is frequently described as one of the primary benefits of participation in faculty development programs (Akerlind & Quinlan, 2001; Austin, 1992; Cox, 2001; Eble & McKeachie, 1985). These findings suggest that convening faculty members through various forums to foster the building of collegial networks is recognized as a powerful point of intervention by faculty developers.

It is also telling that more than one-quarter (26%) of the respondents included "acting as a change agent" as one of the three primary goals that guide their programs. Within the field of faculty development, there has been an increased call for an organizational focus in the profession in response to the changing educational environment. Chism (1998) argues that faculty developers can play a crucial role in helping colleges and universities respond to change, and outlines both the tasks involved and the kinds of skills and characteristics developers will need in order to do this work effectively. Similarly, Lieberman and Guskin (2003) propose that addressing change requires the commitment of a number of groups in institutions and that "among the most important will be the work of faculty development professionals and the centers they lead" (p. 257). Our findings suggest that a significant number of our respondents also believe that faculty developers should position themselves as key players in the new educational environment. The goals of fostering collegiality and acting as a change agent might, in fact, be synergistic. Both involve building alliances and kinships among campus constituencies. Both reflect the prime importance of visioning creatively, planning strategically, identifying support, crossing boundaries, creating linkages, and embracing opportunities for community and change.

While focusing on new roles and tasks, faculty developers continue to fulfill the long-standing goal of providing support to individual faculty members who seek improvement in their teaching effectiveness. Specifically, 17% of respondents indicated that "providing support for faculty experiencing difficulty with their teaching" is one of the three primary purposes of their programs. Since the 1970s, faculty development programs have offered diagnostic assessment of teaching aimed at enhancing instruction. Of course, consultation can assist many instructors—from new instructors who did not have teacher training in graduate school, to mid-career faculty members who are concerned about their declining student ratings, to senior lecturers who have won teaching awards but want to further enhance their performance. Often instructors can choose from a range of individual consultation options to assess their teaching strengths and areas that might merit attention. Consultation processes may include clarification of goals, assessment of teaching and student learning (e.g., review of course materials, early feedback from students, classroom observation and/or videotaping, and classroom assessment tools), analysis of information, and improvement efforts (Angelo & Cross, 1993; Bergquist & Phillips, 1975; Brinko & Menges, 1997; Gillespie, Hilsen, & Wadsworth, 2002; Lewis & Lunde, 2001).

Notably, the senior faculty developers at Canadian universities reported the top three goals guiding their programs as identical to those of their U.S. counterparts: creating a culture of teaching excellence (74%), responding to individual faculty members' needs (56%), and advancing new initiatives in teaching and learning (40%). Other key goals were similar as well: providing support for faculty members who are experiencing difficulties with their teaching (33%), and acting as a change agent within the institution (20%). To conclude, the interaction of primary and secondary goals plays a part in the successful integration of a culture of teaching excellence into the life of any campus.

Institutional differences

Overseers of faculty development programming identified many of the same goals as guiding their centers, but there were strong differences among institutional types regarding the priority of specific goals. For example, 82% of liberal arts college developers thought that creating or sustaining a culture of teaching excellence was one of the top three purposes of their programming efforts, compared to 70% at research/doctoral institutions and 69% at community colleges. Sixty percent of liberal arts developers chose "advancing new initiatives in teaching and learning" as one of their top three goals, compared to the overall average across all institutions of 49%. The consensus among liberal arts developers about the importance of creating and sustaining a culture of teaching excellence may reflect their desire to support the traditional emphasis on good teaching at these schools. This accent on a teaching culture among developers at liberal arts colleges is telling, particularly at a time when more and more institutions of all types are striving to adopt research cultures like those of research universities (Morphew, 2002). A director from a liberal arts college commented, "Faculty development [at a liberal arts college] is different from the research university. The culture supports it." Liberal arts developers also identified fostering collegiality within and among faculty and departments as a primary goal (34%), again reflecting the emphasis on academic community as a core cultural value of liberal arts colleges.

   Twenty-seven percent of the respondents from research and doctoral universities and 33% of the developers at Canadian universities indicated that "providing support to faculty members having difficulty" was one of the top three goals guiding their programs. (They selected this goal as primary more frequently than respondents at other institutional types.) Historically, universities have emphasized research more than teaching in the training, hiring, and rewarding of faculty members. The renewed focus on undergraduate education, however, has placed increasing pressure on research and doctoral universities to develop new faculty as teachers, to enhance the effectiveness of post-tenure faculty, and to assess and reward teaching excellence (Boyer Commission on Educating Undergraduates in the Research University, 1998; Association of American Colleges and Universities, 2002). The goals of teaching and learning centers in research universities are likely to have been shaped in response to such realities and expectations. This finding may reflect the greater capacity of faculty development units in research universities to provide individual consultation in teaching to improve and enhance teaching skills.

Table 2.6: Percent of U.S. Senior Respondents Choosing Goal Among Top Three Primary Goals for Their Program

Goal	All	R/D	Comp	LA	CC
To create or sustain a culture of teaching excellence	72%	70%	75%	82%	69%
To respond to and support individual faculty members	56%	53%	60%	62%	59%
To advance new initiatives in teaching and learning	49%	45%	52%	60%	31%
To foster collegiality within/among faculty/departments	26%	23%	26%	34%	28%
To act as a change agent within the institution	26%	27%	24%	26%	24%
To provide support for faculty members having difficulty	17%	27%	11%	5%	14%
To respond to critical needs of the institution	15%	18%	14%	8%	24%
To provide recognition and reward for excellence in teaching	13%	17%	14%	3%	14%
To position institution at forefront of educational innovation	7%	6%	6%	0%	10%
To support departmental goals, planning, and development	7%	6%	4%	8%	17%

R/D = Research/Doctoral; Comp = Comprehensive; LA = Liberal Arts;
CC = Community College

Least Influential Goals

Goals that the fewest number of respondents chose as primary guiding forces included the following (again, these overall percentages refer to the proportion of senior respondents across all U.S. institutional types who identified the goal as one of the three primary goals for their programs):

- Responding to critical needs as defined by the institution (15%)
- Providing recognition and reward for excellence in teaching (13%)
- Supporting departmental goals and development (7%)
- Positioning the institution at the forefront of educational innovation (7%)

Remarkably, these goals are reported in other parts of the data as among the most important challenges facing institutions that affect faculty work (see Chapter 5, which discusses faculty development challenges). Developers may perceive some of these goals as outside the primary domain of faculty development programs. For example, institutions may have various critical needs that cannot be addressed by faculty development, such as fundraising or handling state-mandated budget cuts. On the other hand, it is clear that developers are prepared to help address critical institutional needs pertaining to teaching and learning issues. Indeed, meeting these challenges will require a collaborative effort on the part of faculty developers, faculty, administrators, and students. In terms of "providing recognition and reward for excellence in teaching," faculty development centers often bestow such recognition through teaching awards, grants, and fellowships, but, when asked to identify primary goals, respondents may perceive this task as a routine or ongoing service and therefore not one of the key goals guiding their programs. Additionally, respondents may have recognized that annual reviews of faculty teaching effectiveness and recognition of teaching in tenure, promotion, and merit decisions are located primarily at the departmental and college levels. Faculty development programs are typically not designed to address personnel policies and practices that are evaluative in nature. Yet how to address the real issue—to what extent teaching should figure into the decisions departments make about faculty appointments, tenure, and promotion—remains an essential question for faculty development.

Similarly, the low percentage of developers selecting "supporting departmental goals, planning, and development" as a primary goal may reflect the field's traditional focus on the needs and interests of individual faculty members rather than on entire units or programs. It may also indicate developers' awareness of the limited resources and time available to broadly support the needs and goals of all departments. Nevertheless, research on faculty development continues to point to the crucial role that department chairs play in setting departmental goals conducive to effective teaching (Donald, 1997; Lucas, 1994, 2002; Wright & O'Neil, 1995). As shown in Chapter 5, respondents do identify academic leadership and management at the departmental level as one of the top five topics faculty development should address.

Community colleges identified responding to "critical needs as defined by the institution" as a guiding goal more often than did other institutions (24%), perhaps representing a shift from the findings that suggested that community college faculty development lacked goals tied to institutional mission (Murray, 2002). Community colleges, by mission, tend to be attuned to external needs and quick to shift educational programs to respond. Further, the traditionally bureaucratic organizational structure of community colleges may make institutional priorities more salient to faculty development programs. A community college faculty developer noted the support for attention to institutional mission: "Faculty development will increasingly reflect institutional goals, priorities, and initiatives."

Senior respondents in Canadian universities identified "providing recognition and reward for excellence in teaching" as a guiding goal (33%) far more often than their U.S. counterparts. Interestingly, an earlier study of Canadian developers, faculty, and administrators found that linking faculty career advancement to teaching performance was perceived as an important avenue to improving teaching. Means to that end included recognition of teaching in tenure and promotion decisions, hiring practices requiring a demonstration of teaching ability, annual review of faculty teaching effectiveness, and use of a teaching dossier to record teaching accomplishments (Wright & O'Neill, 1995).

Conclusion

We hope that this brief summary of how our survey was conducted and the demographic details of its respondents, together with our outline of how institutions currently structure their faculty development programs and what goals and purposes guide program development, will be helpful as readers consider the findings presented in the next three chapters.

Chapter highlights

- Individuals responsible for faculty development often hold more than one title, and the majority are relatively new to the field.

- There has been tremendous growth in centralized units of faculty development across all institutions since the 1970s, yet models and structures remain strongly related to institutional type.

- Primary goals for faculty development programs are remarkably consistent across institutional types, but there are distinct differences by institutional type in the prioritization of specific goals.

3

Influences on Developers and Programs

Faculty development programs often occupy a unique place in the structure of an institution because they serve the entire academic community in the common cause of improving the education that students receive. They are primarily designed to respond to faculty needs—a role that is different from most administrative offices, which respond to students and other constituencies. While they may be first and foremost advocates for faculty in their role as teachers, they are also part of the administration. Ideally, a center should further the agenda for teaching excellence by providing support and service to academic leaders (chairs, deans, and administrators) as well as to faculty—without being perceived as merely an arm of the administration. Program directors and staff must at times be prepared to walk the tightrope in a delicate balancing act, but must also recognize that the center needs the assistance of all these constituencies to build consensus on the best use of its resources.

Influences on Faculty Development Program Goals

Since faculty development programs can be influenced by the priorities of a number of stakeholders, and by issues within and outside of their institutions, we wanted to understand what factors influenced the foci and activities of our respondents' programs. We presented them with a list of eight potential factors that guide programming selections (drawn from our experience in faculty development and current topics in the literature):

- Faculty interests and concerns
- Priorities of department chairs and deans
- Priorities of senior-level institutional leaders
- Priorities of the director or person leading the program
- Immediate organizational issues, concerns, or problems
- Institutional strategic plan
- The faculty development program's strategic plan
- Priorities indicated in higher education or faculty development literature

We asked respondents to indicate the extent to which each factor influenced the focus and activities of the faculty development program at their institution, ranking them on a 4-point Likert-type scale (1 = Not at All; 2 = Slightly Influences; 3 = Moderately Influences; 4 = Greatly Influences; NS = Not Sure). We also gave respondents the option to rate and describe influences that we did not list. The results are listed in Table 3.1.

The highest-rated influences on programming and activities among all developers were:

- Faculty interests and concerns (mean: 3.71)
- Priorities of the director or person leading the program (mean: 3.16)
- Priorities of senior-level administrators (mean: 3.00)

Overwhelmingly, the factor most influencing the foci and activities of our respondents' faculty development efforts were the needs and interests of faculty in their institutions. The influence of "faculty interests and concerns" aligns with our respondents' earlier answer that "responding to faculty members' needs" was the primary goal that guided their programs. Many centers develop ongoing structures for assessing faculty interests and program outcomes through a variety of means such as an advisory committee or faculty interviews, focus groups, and surveys. Such needs assessments and program reviews can be conducted internally or by an external consultant (Sorcinelli, Austin, & Wulff, 2003).

The influence of faculty on developers' priorities is reinforced by studies that indicate that faculty development programs are most effective when they have strong faculty ownership and involvement (Eble & McKeachie 1985; Sorcinelli, 2002), which helps ensure that the program remains responsive to faculty needs. Faculty engagement also provides a channel for the emergence of faculty who can take a leadership role in teaching development and renewal and in student learning. While the director of a center must oversee and guide initiatives, the final product needs to be faculty-inspired.

Not surprisingly, the priorities of the program leader or director were also cited as a primary influence (mean: 3.16). The significant influence of program directors on the direction of programs argues for their ongoing engagement in professional development through reading, attending conferences and other training, and networking.

Respondents were equally well aware of and responsive to the priorities of senior-level institutional leaders (mean: 3.00). An administration that is committed to the concept of faculty development and takes specific actions to create and support a positive environment for teaching is as crucial as faculty involvement (Sorcinelli & Aitken, 1995). Optimally, the administration provides the budgetary support for the faculty development center's staffing and programs. Additionally, senior academic officers give tremendous credibility and visibility to the program by participating in its activities (e.g., programs and award ceremonies) and by naming these activities as important to the institution and its values. The special role that academic administrators can take in fostering faculty development, particularly through symbolic leadership and innovative structures for faculty incentives and rewards, has been well documented (Green, 1990; Seldin & Associates, 1990; Sorcinelli & Aitken, 1995).

Overall, faculty developers were more influenced by the interests and concerns of faculty members and the priorities of senior-level administrators than by the priorities of department chairs and deans, whose influence was only slight to moderate (mean: 2.76). There are several possible reasons for this. Chairs often rotate, so that developers must routinely make time to build relationships with new chairs. It may also be difficult for developers to gain access to chairs, who often feel overwhelmed by paperwork and administrative tasks. Developers might not have skills in the areas of planned change, organizational development, or leadership training, topics that can be of interest to department chairs. Additionally, faculty developers are constrained by limits of time and resources. Nevertheless, departments and colleges within universities often have legitimate priorities that would be well served by the support of faculty development expertise. Academic leaders should also consider how best to meet these needs. Some universities are incorporating department chair and academic leadership training into their faculty development offerings. Two campuses offer successful examples of this approach: Michigan State University's Faculty and Organizational Development Program provides regular department chair workshops throughout the year, and members of the Consortium for Interinstitutional Collaboration (the Big Ten and the University of Chicago) offer a yearlong academic leadership training program for faculty members interested in developing leadership abilities. And at the University of Massachusetts Amherst, the Center for Teaching and provost's office cosponsor an annual deans and chairs conference to allow academic leaders to meet together to address issues of institutional import.

Overall, the least powerful influences on program goals and activities were issues indicated by the literature in higher education and faculty development (mean: 2.64). We suspect that in their day-to-day work, developers spend most of their time responding to and being influenced by faculty members and administrators rather than sorting through the mountains of information available on higher education and faculty development. The literature does strongly influence individual practice (see the following discussion on the effect of pedagogical and faculty development literature on personal practice). This finding may again suggest that faculty developers, much like faculty, already have more priorities and obligations than can be reasonably be met. One developer noted, "I wonder how many faculty development staff find that they, like me, are so busy responding to requests and running successful programs that they have little time to keep up with literatures and organizations." It also suggests that that faculty developers would welcome more avenues and opportunities for scholarly reflection on practice.

Table 3.1: Means of Influences on Faculty Development Programs by Institutional Type

Influence	Total Mean (SD)	R/D Mean (SD)	Comp Mean (SD)	LA Mean (SD)	CC Mean (SD)	Other Mean (SD)
Faculty interests and concerns	3.71 (.62)	3.73 (.57)	3.63 (.68)	3.83 (.49)	3.59 (.91)	3.80 (.41)
Priorities of director or person leading program	3.16 (.87)	3.35 (.65)	3.06 (.95)	3.32 (.79)	2.48 (1.15)	3.07 (.83)
Priorities of senior-level institutional leaders	3.00 (.96)	3.19 (.86)	2.90 (.96)	2.71 (1.02)	2.76 (1.12)	3.20 (1.01)
Immediate organizational issues, concerns, or problems	2.87 (.88)	2.94 (.76)	2.82 (.93)	2.78 (.91)	2.83 (1.00)	2.86 (1.17)
Your faculty development program's strategic plan	2.82 (1.22)	2.80 (1.13)	2.87 (1.29)	2.68 (1.36)	2.72 (1.36)	3.00 (.96)
Priorities of department chairs and dean	2.76 (.87)	2.88 (.84)	2.70 (.88)	2.67 (.82)	2.55 (1.06)	2.53 (.92)
Institutional strategic plan	2.71 (.99)	2.65 (.91)	2.85 (1.04)	2.62 (.88)	2.69 (1.17)	2.27 (1.28)
Priorities from higher education or faculty development literature	2.64 (.87)	2.79 (.78)	2.79 (.82)	2.27 (1.05)	2.17 (.97)	2.80 (.68)
Other influences	3.24 (1.16)	3.30 (1.34)	3.50 (.76)	3.00 (0)	3.50 (.71)	2.33 (2.08)

R/D = Research/Doctoral; Comp = Comprehensive; LA = Liberal Arts;
CC = Community College; 1= Not at All; 2=Slightly Influences;
3= Moderately Influences; 4= Greatly Influences

Institutional differences

The rating of the relative importance of various factors influencing faculty development programs is quite similar at different institutional types; moreover, respondents across institutional types rated faculty interests and concerns as the strongest influence on their programs. At research and comprehensive universities and liberal arts colleges, the second strongest influence was the "priorities of the director or person leading the program." In contrast, the priorities of the director or the person leading the program were rated as less influential at community colleges than at the other institutions (mean: 2.48). As noted earlier, faculty development structures in community colleges rely as much on individuals, committees, and clearinghouses to set priorities as they do on directors in central units.

Influences on Individual Practice of Faculty Development

While it is useful to understand the goals that guide and the factors that influence faculty development programs, it is equally important to understand the sources from which faculty developers derive their ideas. We asked respondents to indicate the extent to which a number of potential sources of information—research, networking, and professional development provided through literature and organizations—contributed to their ideas about faculty development practice. Respondents rated the influence of a list of possible sources (which included various publications and associations) on a 4-point Likert-type scale with 4 indicating the greatest influence (1 = Not at All; 2 = Contributes Slightly; 3 = Contributes Moderately; 4 = Contributes Greatly). We again included a space where respondents could write in other sources.

Overall, faculty developers across institutional types agreed on the most important influences on their practice. (The results of their responses are summarized in Appendix 2, Table A.) They reported that they were influenced more by literature than by either professional or scholarly organizations.

The literature developers were asked to assess pertained to the following topics:

- Higher education
- College teaching and learning
- Adult and continuing education
- Human resources/personal development
- Faculty development (e.g., the POD Network) literature
- Organizational development
- Disciplinary teaching journals

Faculty development literature has burgeoned over the last decade with the advent of new newsletters, journals, and handbooks on teaching, learning, and faculty motivation and development. Menges, Weimer, and Associates (1996) argue that such new scholarship can inform the practice of instruction, increase the value of teaching for those who do it, and promote changes in the faculty role, largely in response to new realities and challenges. The literature also shows that critical new findings can inform and enhance day-to-day practice not only in the classroom but also in faculty development centers.

Developers found that the literature on college teaching and learning (mean: 3.64), the literature in faculty development, such as the POD Network's annual edited volume *To Improve the Academy* (mean: 3.47), and the literature in higher education (mean: 3.36) contributed most to their ideas about faculty development and influenced their practice. They rely primarily on literature that can help them and the faculty members with whom they work to think more creatively and systematically about teaching and learning processes. Such literature can include guidelines for planning, providing, evaluating, and improving instruction, as well as the results of research on learners and the learning process. Similarly, the literature in faculty development and in higher education can provide useful resources on faculty development programs, career development, development as teachers, development as individuals, and organizational development. Canadian developers are influenced more by the literature in adult and continuing education (mean: 3.03) than developers in any of the U.S. institutional types, perhaps due to the robust Canadian literature and research base in this domain and the quality of adult-centered colleges and universities in Canada (Mancuso, 2001).

The respondents were also asked to use the same scale to rate the influence of various associations on their thinking and practice (results are listed in Appendix 2, Table A). Those associations included:

- American Association for Higher Education (AAHE)
- American Association for Adult and Continuing Education (AAACE)
- American Association of Community Colleges (AACC)
- American Educational Research Association (AERA)
- Association for the Study of Higher Education (ASHE)
- American Society for Training and Development (ASTD)
- Professional and Organizational Development Network in Higher Education (POD Network)
- Disciplinary or interdisciplinary associations
- Regional faculty development consortia

Overall, faculty developers tap into the intellectual and collegial resources of two key organizations: the POD Network (mean: 3.41) and AAHE (mean: 3.11). As noted earlier, the POD Network was founded in direct response to the need expressed by faculty members, administrators, and others working in the field of faculty development for a source of professional information and support. The POD Network provides support through publications, conferences, consulting, and networking. It also fulfills an advocacy role at a national level, seeking to inform and persuade educational leaders of the value of faculty development in institutions of higher education (Gillespie, Hilsen, & Wadsworth, 2002). The findings confirm the overwhelming contribution the POD Network makes to faculty developers across institutional types. Admittedly, since only POD Network members were surveyed, a heightened awareness of its services and contributions was perhaps to be expected.

Faculty developers, particularly those in research, comprehensive, and liberal arts institutions, have also apparently found a second home in AAHE. Throughout the 1990s, AAHE hosted an annual Forum on Faculty Roles and Rewards attended by large numbers of administrators, faculty across the disciplines, faculty developers, and staff. AAHE conferences and publications have also addressed issues critical to academic affairs and American undergraduate reform agendas—teaching, learning, curriculum, assessment, diversity, faculty roles, and the pedagogic aspects of technology (DeZure, 2000). The POD Network and AAHE have enjoyed a long-standing collaborative relationship. For example, the POD Network's board of directors meets just prior to the AAHE annual conference. In turn, AAHE staff members have often been invited to present at the POD Network's annual conference. AAHE has also called upon POD Network officers and members to serve as senior scholars, to offer pre-conference workshops, and to work on special projects.

Institutional differences

Respondents from community colleges were more influenced by "other organizations," a category many identified as NCSPOD, which is affiliated with the POD Network. These developers also mentioned the influence of the American Association of Community Colleges (AACC) more than respondents from other institutional types, indicating that AACC slightly to moderately contributed to their ideas about faculty development (mean: 2.60).

Canadian respondents reported being influenced by regional faculty development consortia (mean: 3.13) far more than did U.S. respondents from across institutional types. Factors of size, geography, language, and culture help to account for the influence of regional consortia among Canadian developers. For example, faculty development professionals in Canada met informally for a number of years at universities across the provinces prior to forming a national faculty development organization, the Society for Teaching and Learning in Higher Education (STLHE), thus developing strong networks within as well as among the provinces. As noted in Chapter 1, Canadian developers continue to provide highly regarded forums for the exchange of ideas on post-secondary teaching and learning at the regional and national levels through STLHE.

The modest influence of regional faculty development consortia reported by U.S. respondents was somewhat surprising. There is a wide range of well-regarded regional consortia (e.g., the Great Plains Regional Consortium on Instructional Development, the Historically Black Colleges and Universities [HBCU] Faculty Development Network, the Southern Regional Faculty and Instructional Development Consortium, the New England Faculty Development Consortium) that direct their efforts toward exchanging information on faculty and instructional development through web sites, newsletters, annual conferences, and other activities. National and international associations such as the POD Network and AAHE are characterized by greater capacity and resources than regional networks. The ability of these associations to engage multiple constituencies, institutions, and stakeholders in higher education in multiple ways (e.g., envisioning and articulating national agendas for change, convening forums of opinion leaders, collaborating with organizations engaged in complementary work, and disseminating knowledge on teaching, learning, and academic careers) may contribute to their greater influence on thinking and practice.

Differences by experience

When the ratings of influences on faculty development practices were examined by the primary title of the respondent, a number of interesting differences emerged. Senior administrators rated AAHE and literature in higher education more highly than the POD Network or literature in faculty development. They differed in this from directors, assistant and associate directors, and midlevel administrators, who rely more heavily on the latter sources. Senior administrators might rely on AAHE because one of its primary focuses is on building the leadership capacity of academic administrators and envisioning and articulating agendas for change in higher education. Similarly, the broad literature in higher education may speak more to systemic improvement in higher education, while the POD Network and faculty development literature focus more on contributing to and disseminating the body of knowledge on teaching, learning, academic career development, and faculty development practices.

When examining the ratings in terms of faculty developers' years of experience, we saw that experienced developers (those with more than 10 years of experience) rated many influences more highly than did new developers (5 or fewer years of experience). It appears that although the two groups agree in primary influences, they differ in secondary influences. More experienced faculty developers seem to draw on a wider range of research and literature, and on resources in adult and continuing education and personal and organizational development—areas that new developers did not note as influential. Experienced developers also seem to have more awareness of and connections to a wider range of professional associations, particularly research-intensive associations such as AERA and ASHE.

Model Programs

Because we wanted to know which faculty development programs respondents perceived as offering successful approaches to faculty development, we asked, "Faculty development programs are sometimes influenced by ideas that have been implemented in other institutions' programs. What other programs in faculty development have served as models for your efforts or influenced your program?" Each respondent was invited to list up to three institutions or programs that influenced his or her practice.

Overall, our respondents named 158 different institutions and programs as models or exemplars and identified over 80 research and doctoral institutions, almost 30 comprehensive universities, 30 liberal arts colleges, 7 community colleges, and a number of specialized colleges, programs, and systems as meritorious. Sixty-five of these institutions were named by two or more respondents. These responses suggest that faculty developers look to a wide variety of other institutions and programs for inspiration.

A small number of institutions had the distinction of being named most often as models by developers across every institutional type—from community colleges to research universities. They were, in alphabetical order, Miami University of Ohio, University of Delaware, University of Massachusetts Amherst, and University of Michigan.

While long-established programs at research and doctoral institutions tended to be named most, developers named distinctive faculty development programs at every institutional type. Model programs most cited at research universities included (in alphabetical order) Harvard University, Miami University of Ohio, Ohio State University, Stanford University, University of Delaware, University of Massachusetts Amherst, University of Michigan, University of North Carolina–Chapel Hill, University of Texas–Austin, and University of Washington. Model programs most often cited at comprehensive universities were: Appalachian State University, Portland State University, and the University of Central Florida. Among liberal arts colleges, the most frequently mentioned programs were those at Alverno College, King's College, and St. Norbert College. At community colleges, developers most often identified programs at the Community College of Aurora and Maricopa Community College. Canadian universities most often cited included Queens University, University of Alberta, the University of British Columbia, and University of Manitoba. (Readers are encouraged to visit the POD Network web site, http://www.podnetwork.org, for links to many of these faculty development programs.)

Given the diversity of these responses, we then cross-referenced programs identified by faculty developers with the list of winners of the Theodore M. Hesburgh Award for Faculty Development to Enhance Undergraduate Teaching and Learning. This annual award recognizes three to five colleges or universities, selected through a rigorous two-stage evaluation process by readers and a panel of national experts in faculty development initiatives. (Readers from the POD Network, the Council of Independent Colleges, and AACC and its affiliate, NCSPOD, assist in the preliminary evaluation of the entries. For more information see TIAA-CREF Institute's web site, http://www.tiaa-crefinstitute.org/Awards/awardp2.htm.) There was considerable overlap (see Table 3.2): 16 of the institutions identified by developers were also included among the 61 recipients of the Hesburgh Award from 1993–2004 (see Appendix 3 for a complete listing). Taken together, the identification of faculty development programs that model best practices and the cross-reference of these programs with Hesburgh Award winners suggest that innovation and achievement in faculty development are recognized both by professional peers and by experts in higher education.

Conclusion

Our survey demonstrates the wide range of sources that influence the individual practices of faculty development professionals and the goals of their programs. The concerns of faculty members and the priorities of program directors and institutions' senior administrators ranked most highly among influences on programming and activities. Indeed, it has been suggested that in determining issues to address and priorities to set, a program stands a better chance if it is designed in direct response to the concerns of all constituencies—faculty, administrators, and students (Sorcinelli, 2002). In the next two chapters, we look at how developers identify and prioritize the key issues and challenges that face their institutions now and those that are likely to affect faculty work in the coming years.

Table 3.2: Institutions Identified as Models That Also Received Hesburgh Awards

Institution	Year	Title of Program
Alverno College	1994	Faculty as Scholars of Teaching
Indiana University–Bloomington	2003	Scholarship of Teaching and Learning Project
Indiana University–Purdue University Indianapolis	2002	Gateway Program to Enhance Student Retention
King's College (PA)	1995	Faculty Development and Student Learning Assessment
Miami University of Ohio	1994 2003	The Teaching Scholars Program Faculty Learning Community
Portland State University	2002	Community-University Partnership Program
Syracuse University	1993	Future Professoriate Project
University of California–Berkeley	1994	American Cultures Program
University of California–Los Angeles	2004	Freshman Cluster Program
University of Delaware	1999	Problem Based Learning
University of Massachusetts Amherst	2000	Building Community: Creating Campus Change
University of Michigan	1996 2000	Undergraduate Research Opportunities Program / Program on Intergroup Relations, Conflict, and Community
University of Missouri–Columbia	1997	The General Education Program
University of South Carolina	1997	The Integrated Undergraduate Faculty Development Program
University of Washington	1993	Entry Level Initiative
University of Wisconsin System	2001	Women and Science Program

Chapter highlights

- Across institutional types, faculty development programs and practices are most influenced by the interests and concerns of faculty members, literature on college teaching and learning, and the POD Network.

- Experienced faculty developers tend to be influenced by a wider range of literature and organizations than are new developers.

- A number of colleges and universities across institutional types with recognized faculty development programs serve as models of best practice for their peers.

4

Current Issues Addressed by Faculty Development Services

T he world of higher education has changed considerably since faculty development programs first emerged in the 1960s. Approaches to teaching and learning have been no exception; DeZure (2000) catalogues a wide range of topics, such as new instructional approaches, innovative technologies, a commitment to diversity, and assessment of teaching and student learning outcomes. She suggests that "these changes were propelled not by a single engine, but by many different developments acting as levers—shaping attitudes, creating opportunities, promoting shifts in policies and practices" (p. 4).

We wondered which key issues and changes were currently being addressed by faculty development programs and services. While earlier studies have described the kinds of resources and services that are characteristic of the field, ours is the first study to ask developers about the major issues that undergird the array of services offered through their faculty development programs. This chapter presents the important issues identified in teaching, learning, and faculty work that developers currently address—or do not address—in their programs.

Current Issues and New Challenges

We queried faculty developers with a list of 21 "current issues" and a second list of 17 "new challenges and pressures" regarding teaching, learning, and other aspects of faculty work. The items were culled from a review of the literature on current faculty and institutional issues and from previous reports documenting faculty development center offerings. Arguably, some of the items included in the list of current issues might have been considered new challenges and vice versa. However, the current issues tended to be areas that we perceived as being emphasized by faculty development programs at the time of our survey. For example, "multiculturalism and diversity related to teaching" was included as a current issue, since the topic had been discussed in the faculty development literature in the years preceding our survey and a number of institutions have developed programs to help faculty address this issue. On the other hand, "balancing multiple faculty roles" was included in our survey as a new challenge since we were not aware of a large number of institutions already addressing this issue through programming.

Respondents used 4-point Likert-type scales (1 = Not at All; 2 = To a Slight Extent; 3 = To a Moderate Extent; 4 = To a Great Extent; NS = Not Sure) to assess each current issue in terms of whether it is addressed through faculty development services and the extent to which they believe it is important for their faculty development program to offer services pertaining to the item. Similarly, respondents assessed each item on the list of new challenges and pressures in terms of whether the institution offers relevant services and resources and the extent to which the item should be addressed through faculty development. They could also specify other services that they currently offered or believed important to address. (Table B and Table C in Appendix 2 provide a list of all items with mean ratings and standard deviations.)

This chapter offers a portrait of key current issues that are being addressed through faculty development services and which of these current issues faculty developers believe are most important to address. The chapter also opens consideration of possible new issues concerning faculty work for institutions to address and which of these issues developers think should be addressed through faculty development. In analyzing the overall findings, we discovered that although faculty developers provide services for the issues they believe important, they do not provide them to an extent commensurate with the degree to which they considered the issues important. This suggests that the capacity of faculty development programs to address key issues and provide important services does not match the perceived need. This pattern was prevalent for all ranges of responses, from issues identified as the least to the most important to address.

Despite often limited resources and capacity, many faculty development programs have engaged creatively with the key issues in teaching, learning, and other aspects of faculty work. They have shared innovative practices, particularly through the Professional and Organizational Development Network in Higher Education (POD Network) conferences and publications. Some faculty development programs have been further recognized as models of best practice at a national level through the Hesburgh Award. As noted earlier, the goal of the Hesburgh Award is to acknowledge and reward successful, innovative faculty development programs that enhance undergraduate teaching and help to inspire the growth of such initiatives at other colleges and universities. Our discussions of the key issues that developers identified as highly important to address highlight some of the programs that have been recognized for their responsiveness to these issues.

Faculty Developers' Views: Key Issues and Current Services

Developers identified eight current issues they believed to be most important *and* that their programs currently address. Each of these issues was rated by developers as important to offer by faculty development programs to at least a moderate extent (mean: 3.00 or more) and rated as currently offered between a slight and a moderate extent (mean: 2.50 or more). Following the list of the eight issues, we discuss the possible reasons why each is important and how programs attend to them.

Table 4.1: Mean Ratings of Key Issues That Are Important to Offer and Currently Offered

Issue	Important to Offer	Currently Offered
Teaching for student-centered learning	3.69	3.25
New faculty development	3.60	3.03
Integrating technology into traditional teaching and learning settings	3.51	3.28
Active, inquiry-based, or problem-based learning	3.51	3.00
Assessment of student learning outcomes	3.43	2.57
Multiculturalism and diversity related to teaching	3.36	2.75
Scholarship of Teaching	3.28	2.57
Writing Across the Curriculum	3.06	2.46

Teaching for student-centered learning

Developers identified teaching for student-centered learning as *the most important issue* to address through services for faculty (mean: 3.69) and they currently offer services related to this issue to an impressive extent (mean: 3.25). Student-centered learning has been an important topic since teaching development literature (McKeachie, 2002) began, and in the last decade many more higher education researchers and practitioners have called for a shift from a teacher-centered paradigm to one focused on student learning (Barr & Tagg, 1995; Johnson, Johnson, & Smith, 1991, 1998). Thus it is not surprising that this topic is high on the agenda when faculty developers consider the issues their programs should address. As one faculty developer in a liberal arts college commented, "Faculty development should be preparing faculty to think differently about teaching—to enable them to move away from primarily lecture (knowledge-dissemination) to learning orientation (facilitation)." A center director from a research university highlighted the growing complexities of learner-centered teaching: "As always, faculty development must help faculty members prepare for excellence in teaching—with a focus on excellence in student learning. That goal and process is far more comprehensive and complicated than it was twenty years ago—or as we addressed it twenty years ago."

Teaching for student-centered learning does not imply a single method of teaching. It emphasizes a range of classroom methods that shift the teacher's role from dispenser of information to facilitator of student learning. It also encompasses learning that occurs outside of the classroom, such as community service-learning, internships, and study abroad. Researchers and practitioners in faculty development have studied, created, and shared initiatives in such arenas as problem-based service-learning, learning groups, student learning communities, and teaching for higher-level learning (Chickering & Gamson, 1991; Fink, 2003; France, 2004; Reynolds, 2003). A community college developer suggested that student-centered teaching is time-intensive and necessitates the cultivation of new skills and attitudes among faculty and faculty developers: "In the past, many of our faculty could develop basic instructional skills over time. However, the shift to learner-centered instruction, increased use of technologies, and the changing role of instructors makes training in sound instructional basics challenging and absolutely essential." Several Hesburgh Award programs have been designed around student-centered learning.

- *Babson College, 2000 Hesburgh Award Winner.* Babson College adopted the goal of better preparing students for working in the 21st century—as interdisciplinary thinkers capable of self-directed learning. When faculty saw that this goal could be achieved only by changing how they taught fundamental business practices, over one-third of Babson's full-time faculty joined in a project to revise the curriculum and the methods of teaching it.

- *University of South Carolina, 1997 Hesburgh Certificate of Excellence Winner.* Three general principles redefined the University of South Carolina's thinking about faculty development: Faculty development should be closely linked with enhanced student learning, more intellectual contact should be fostered between undergraduates and faculty outside the classroom, and the university should facilitate more intellectual experiences in common for faculty and students. New initiatives included a University 101 faculty development program, college-specific freshman seminars, faculty development grants, and faculty mentors for freshman scholarship winners.

- *Syracuse University, 1996 Hesburgh Award Winner.* In the Transformation to a Student-Centered Research University Program, Syracuse University underwent several campus initiatives and rebalanced its priorities of teaching and scholarship. Introductory courses were revised to emphasize computer and critical thinking skills, small recitation sections and freshman seminars were adopted, and a comprehensive mid-semester progress report system was created to identify and support students who were struggling academically.

New faculty development

Overall, developers identified new faculty development as a critically important area to address in terms of programming (mean: 3.60) and one of the top three issues for which they offer services (mean: 3.03). A community college program coordinator commented: "Faculty development should concentrate on the recruitment, hiring, and professional (educational) training for our new generation of academically talented faculty."

The priority of this issue among developers across institutional types is likely the result of the changing demographics and composition of faculty ranks due to retirements and the proliferation of new areas of study that have necessitated the hiring of large numbers of new faculty. As early as 1992, new full-time faculty at institutions of higher education comprised one-third of the full-time faculty ranks (Finkelstein, Seal, & Schuster, 1998a). In addition, studies of graduate students and new faculty indicate that they desire more support in acclimating to the culture of the institution, figuring out expectations for performance, finding mentors, and balancing work and life outside of work (Rice, Sorcinelli, & Austin, 2000). A liberal arts college director noted: "We need to do a better job of 'courting' good Ph.D. candidates, keeping newly trained faculty, and not treating these instructors badly."

Researchers and practitioners in faculty development have suggested a wide variety of good practices for improving the life of new and early career faculty (Boice, 1992; Menges & Associates, 1999; Rice, Sorcinelli, & Austin, 2000; Sorcinelli, 2000; Sorcinelli & Austin, 1992; Tierney & Bensimon, 1996; Trower, 2000). Many faculty development programs do offer services and strategies to support new faculty development. These range from new faculty orientations, web sites that offer new faculty survival guides, grants to assist newcomers with scholarship and teaching, mentoring programs, teaching fellow programs, training for department chairs, and academic networks for dual-career couples.

Respondents from research and doctoral institutions showed the largest disparity between the extent to which they offered services to newcomers (mean: 2.90) and their ranking of new faculty development as an important issue to address (mean: 3.59). This may reflect the sheer numbers of graduate teaching assistants (TAs) and new faculty who arrive at most research universities with little pedagogical training. A research university director observed: "A major underlying reality affecting present faculty (and which may continue for a while) is the lack of pedagogical preparation along with discipline specialization. Too many new faculty are lacking in basic skills areas such as course design, syllabus development, learning theory, etc."

New faculty development has been addressed in the following innovative Hesburgh Award programs.

- *Georgia Institute of Technology, 1999 Hesburgh Certificate of Excellence Winner.* At Georgia Institute of Technology, an alumni-funded teaching program focused on cohorts of new faculty and provided them with weekly teaching seminars, feedback from the Center for the Enhancement of Teaching and Learning staff and students, and the guidance of mentors. Programs for graduate TAs and senior faculty also were implemented; all are permanently endowed.

- *University of Maryland–Eastern Shore and Salisbury State University, 1998 Hesburgh Certificate of Excellence Winners.* In a two-campus Collaborative New Faculty Initiative Program, a Historically Black University (the University of Maryland–Eastern Shore) and a traditional non-minority university (Salisbury State University) pooled their expertise and resources to help their newest faculty members achieve success in their academic careers. The program sought to improve classroom teaching skills, enabled participants to develop collaborative teaching and research projects, and integrated new faculty into the academic community.

- *Miami University of Ohio, 1994 Hesburgh Award Winner.* The Teaching Scholars Program at Miami University of Ohio has fostered teaching excellence by providing guidance in the formative years of junior faculty through seminars on teaching and learning, faculty mentors, individual teaching projects, retreats, national conferences, and a teaching scholarship journal.

Integrating technology into traditional teaching and learning settings

Integrating technology into the educational process has become both a challenge and a major initiative for most colleges and universities. Overall, developers recognized the importance of teaching with technology (mean: 3.51), and this issue received the highest rating in terms of services offered (mean: 3.28). A community college director noted: "Faculty development should support the appropriate, effective, and innovative use of evolving, mainstream instructional technologies that support students wherever they are—be it in a classroom, on campus, in transit, at home, or at work."

When considering technology in their teaching, many instructors begin with questions about various tools such as PowerPoint, email, the Internet, and online courseware. But faculty developers support the appropriate and effective use of technology by asking faculty to step back and take a more systematic approach to the integration of technology in their courses. Zhu and Kaplan (2002) suggest that developers should help faculty members examine various factors involved in the teaching and learning process: "The successful integration of technology entails the careful consideration of course content, the capabilities of various technology tools, student access to and comfort with technology, and the instructor's view of his or her role in the teaching and learning process" (p. 221).

The work of faculty developers is increasingly impacted by technology, not only as developers help faculty solve the challenges of integrating technology into teaching, but also as they integrate teaching technologies into the organizational structures of their institutions. A number of programs have created linkages among the domains of teaching, learning, and technology through grants, yearlong fellowships, institutes, and workshops (Bellows & Danos, 2003; Rutherford, 2002; Shih & Sorcinelli, 2000). Faculty developers are also helping to articulate how technology, particularly computer-mediated forms, is transforming what it means to teach, learn, and develop faculty (Courtney, 2001; Gillespie, 1998).

Indeed, developers reported that there was a relative match between their capacity to provide services to integrate technology into teaching (mean: 3.28) and the importance of such services (mean: 3.51). Since only a small fraction (1%) of developers identified their primary title as "technology coordinator," this suggests that developers with broad expertise in teaching and learning processes are quite successful in providing services or linking faculty to the appropriate services that can support them in incorporating technology into their classroom experiences. The cautionary message prevalent in responses we received to the open-ended survey questions, however, was that technology training had the potential to dwarf other important development issues (see Chapter 6). A comprehensive university director summarized such concerns: "Technology *is* an important issue and an important support for faculty development and pedagogy, and it should be. But, if faculty development becomes interested only in how and not in what, why, or to whom and for whom, it will be lost."

There are a number of approaches institutions can use to integrate technology into traditional teaching and learning settings, as demonstrated by the following award-winning programs.

- *LaGuardia Community College/City University of New York, 2004 Hesburgh Certificate of Excellence Winner.* Designed for Learning at LaGuardia Community College is an intensive, yearlong professional development process in which faculty use interactive digital technology to engage students, advance their academic success, and enhance their ability to work, think, and lead.

- *Virginia Polytechnic Institute, 1997 Hesburgh Certificate of Excellence Winner.* The Faculty Development Institute at Virginia Polytechnic Institute provided faculty the opportunity to rethink instruction through technology. It concentrated on improving core curriculum courses, offering 58 customized faculty workshops and 47 different sessions on information technology literacy for new students.

- *University of Arizona, 1995 Hesburgh Certificate of Excellence Winner.* The University of Arizona incorporated technology into the undergraduate curriculum and transformed the way math was taught, with dramatic results in student success. The project included making the technology accessible to both faculty and students, and training faculty in different teaching methods facilitated by technology.

Active, inquiry-based, or problem-based learning

Faculty developers across institutional types are aggressively addressing the topic of active learning through services offered (mean: 3.00) and indicated to an even greater extent that such services were important to offer (mean: 3.51). Active learning engages students with content in ways that develop competencies and skills—rather than leading *solely* to the acquisition of knowledge. Some of the major characteristics associated with active-learning strategies include: getting students involved in more than just listening and taking notes, engaging students in activities (e.g., reading, discussing, and writing), often with one another, developing students' higher-order thinking skills (analysis, synthesis, evaluation), and placing greater emphasis on students' exploration of attitudes and values and less emphasis on transmitting information (Sutherland & Bonwell, 1996).

A review of teaching and learning center web sites indicates that a number of programs offer guidance on strategies and methods to facilitate active learning. These include individual consultation, workshops, print resources, and videographies (lists of best videos) to support faculty in teaching students to learn through writing, reading, cases, simulations, and cooperative, peer, problem-based, or inquiry-based work. A number of key resources, many written by directors of teaching and learning centers, also assist faculty developers in learning about and supporting the use of multiple forms of active learning (Bonwell & Eison, 1991; Fink, 2003; Lee, 2004; Michaelsen, Knight, & Fink, 2002; Millis & Cottell, 1998; Weimer, 2002).

Faculty developers at research and doctoral institutions reported that they offered programs on active learning to a greater extent than did developers at comprehensive universities or liberal arts and community colleges. There may be a connection between the interest in active learning at research and doctoral institutions and the growing number of large lecture classes and the concomitant potential for student passivity at such institutions. Faculty development units at the latter three institutional types offered programs on active-learning techniques only to a slight or moderate extent. One developer admitted: "Much remains to be done in active learning, problem-based learning, inquiry learning, and other instructional approaches that lead to better learning. Acceptance is related to institutional change as well as reprioritizing rewards in academe. Nonetheless, real change begins with individuals, so that work should not be neglected."

Model programs in problem-based and active learning have been developed at several institutions.

- *University of Delaware, 1999 Hesburgh Award Winner.* In a faculty-driven reform of the undergraduate experience, many courses at the University of Delaware now utilize problem-based learning in order to motivate students to discover important concepts for themselves while working in teams. The Institute for Transforming Undergraduate Education trained faculty to implement active and problem-based learning.

Fellows of the institute received hands-on experience in employing these strategies, as well as individual mentoring from faculty experienced with these techniques.

- *Rose-Hulman Institute of Technology, 1997 Hesburgh Certificate of Excellence Winner.* Rose-Hulman Institute of Technology designed an Integrated First-Year Curriculum in Science, Engineering, and Mathematics. The program helped prepare students to integrate knowledge between disciplines, to create problem solving strategies, and to learn more effectively in teams. Part of this process included creating an interdisciplinary faculty team to shape the program, integrating technology throughout the learning environment, and emphasizing cooperative learning.

- *Rensselaer Polytechnic Institute, 1995 Hesburgh Award Winner.* Through the use of faculty, graduate student, and undergraduate student teams, Rensselaer Polytechnic Institute's Center for Innovation in Undergraduate Education restructured many introductory courses to integrate studio classes in place of large lecture formats. This resulted in more active learning, a stronger relationship between the course and the laboratory, and emphasis on team and cooperative learning. It also allowed a stronger integration of technology into the structure of courses and the learning environment.

Assessing student learning outcomes

Developers who participated in our survey identified the assessment of student learning outcomes as an important service for their programs to offer. For example, a research university senior administrator stated: "Faculty developers will need to be better grounded in assessment literature and practice." However, the gap between the perceived importance of providing services in support of assessment versus the extent to which such services are actually offered was the most pronounced among the top teaching and learning issues (important to offer, mean: 3.43; currently offering, mean: 2.57).

Across postsecondary education, there has been a growing demand for student learning assessment. In general, however, legislators, higher education boards, accrediting agencies, and administrators have been more enthusiastic about assessment than faculty members. Indeed, until recently much assessment has been at the institutional level, focusing on issues of external accountability or program review rather than on developing assessment activities that help individual faculty members improve their own teaching and student learning.

This is changing. For example, there are a number of practical handbooks that help college faculty develop a better understanding of the learning process in their own classrooms and assess the impact of their teaching on it. They feature classroom assessment techniques and advice on how to adapt and administer the techniques, analyze the data, and implement improvements in teaching and learning practices (Angelo, 1998; Angelo & Cross, 1993; Stassen, Doherty, & Poe, 2001; Walvoord & Anderson, 1998). A review of *To Improve the Academy, Volume 23* includes a full section on strategies for assessing faculty and student learning (Wehlburg & Chadwick-Blossey, 2004).

In their comments, developers suggested reasons for the gap between their rating of the importance of student learning assessment and actual services offered. For example, a comprehensive university administrator acknowledged that assessment is increasingly being used to measure institutional accountability and assign rewards, rather than to assist faculty in clarifying teaching goals and understanding student needs: "Knowledge of student outcomes assessments will continue to be required for our accreditations, performance funding, and faculty pay/rewards." Nonetheless, the responses of developers also indicated that they are well aware of the potential for assessment to make the learning process for individual students more effective and of their responsibility in realizing that potential. A community college program coordinator predicted: "We will see continued work in the assessment of student learning and begin to incorporate this into our [own classroom] teaching." Successful approaches to assessing student learning outcomes include the following programs.

- *Florida Community College at Jacksonville, 1995 Hesburgh Certificate of Excellence Winner.* Working to "bridge the gap between abstract educational research theory and actual day-to-day classroom practices," volunteer faculty at Florida Community College at Jacksonville developed the Center for the Advancement of Teaching and Learning. Projects focused on using the classroom as a modern laboratory for conducting experiments to gauge the impact of teaching on student learning. To achieve this goal, the center sponsored classroom research mini-grants, classroom research, cooperative learning, adjunct faculty development, faculty workshops, and a range of programs concerning student development and support.

- *King's College, 1995 Hesburgh Certificate of Excellence Winner.* King's College designed a Faculty Development and Student Learning Assessment program. The goal was twofold: to measure student learning and to improve it through teaching strategies and criteria. Teams of faculty learned about the best criteria for evaluating student learning, communicating expectations to students, and innovative teaching and learning strategies to help students achieve those goals.

- *Virginia Union University, 1993 Hesburgh Certificate of Excellence Winner.* The Faculty Development Program at Virginia Union University encouraged faculty to expand scholarly endeavors that would have an impact on the educational environment for students. Major components included on-campus programs designed to enhance teaching skills, individual grants for faculty—particularly those activities that would have a widespread impact in assessment—and a journal for sharing scholarly and pedagogical innovation.

Multiculturalism and diversity related to teaching

Developers across institutional types indicated that multiculturalism should be an integral component of their teaching-development services. That this issue was ranked as one of the eight most important current issues to address indicates that faculty developers recognize that their programs can respond to changing demographics on campus and beyond, and can support a campus climate that values diverse ideas, beliefs, and worldviews, promotes community, and cultivates more inclusive student learning environments.

Traditionally, many campuses were slow to incorporate multiculturalism into their faculty development programs. One reason was that institutions tended to focus such efforts on students, suggesting that diversity concerns are a student-development rather than a teaching-development issue. Second, many faculty and graduate student TAs have been reticent about addressing issues of diversity in the classroom because of a lack of training. Third, initiating diversity programming is risky; discussions on many campuses have been clouded by unskillful or inadequate prior efforts (Cook & Sorcinelli, 1999; Ouellett & Sorcinelli, 1995).

For these reasons, there was a great disparity between how developers assessed the importance of offering services pertaining to multiculturalism and the extent of services currently being offered (important to offer, mean: 3.36; currently offering, mean: 2.75). Faculty developers seemed well aware of the gap. A liberal arts college developer suggested: "We should be working toward helping faculty prepare students for life and work in a culturally diverse environment." A research university faculty member added: "Faculty developers need to focus [more] on the realities of changing student demographics—how this will impact the culture of the diverse classroom and to support faculty in this endeavor."

A growing number of faculty development programs are infusing diversity awareness into programs and services. These include workshops and intensive seminars on teaching in the diverse classroom, grants for multicultural projects, occasional papers, and annotated bibliographies on the linkage between teaching, learning, and diversity (Cook & Sorcinelli, 1999). The POD Network has articulated a key goal of becoming a more multicultural organization. It hosts an active Diversity Commission, the goals of which are focused on the recruitment and retention of members from underrepresented groups and institutions. The commission sponsors several initiatives to increase attention to diversity-related issues in the organization that include travel grants to assist faculty developers from underrepresented groups to attend the POD Network conference and support for internships for persons of color who wish to explore career development opportunities in faculty development (Ouellett & Stanley, 2004; Stanley, 2002; Stanley & Ouellett, 2000).

Hesburgh Award programs that address multiculturalism and diversity include:

- *Prince George's Community College, 2002 Hesburgh Certificate of Excellence Winner.* The Book Bridge Project at Prince George's Community College engages faculty and their ethnically and racially diverse students in teaching and learning about sensitive issues of gender, religion, race, and ethnicity by using literary works to bridge barriers. Thirty percent of faculty constitute a core of sustained involvement in the development and implementation of classroom and community-based activities. Faculty develop readers' guides for classroom and community use, engage in collaborative discussions, and participate in campus-wide forums, public school classrooms, and community events.

- *Community College of Denver, 2000 Hesburgh Award Winner.* At the Community College of Denver, the Teaching/Learning Center Program, which included all college employees, had an initial goal of measurably increasing the recruitment, retention, and graduation rates of students of color. Faculty conducted programs, designed evaluations, and guided the teaching and learning center through an advisory committee. The focus of the program has evolved from integrating diversity to an expanded focus on learning-centered instruction. All faculty are required to complete a certain number of hours in the program.

- *Loyola Marymount University, 1998 Hesburgh Award Winner.* The goal of the Growing Together as a Multicultural Community Program at Loyola Marymount University was to help overcome racial and ethnic divisiveness by supporting a diverse, multicultural faculty and student body through an innovative American Cultures course that comparatively studied three of the five major ethnic and racial groups in the U.S. in an interdisciplinary way. A major component of this program was the appointment of faculty of color and the support of graduate students of color.

Scholarship of teaching

Developers from all types of institutions agreed that the scholarship of teaching is an important issue to be addressed in faculty development services (mean: 3.28), although services provided were much more modest (mean: 2.57). One comprehensive university faculty member declared, "We should emphasize the 'scholarship of teaching/learning' to promote the integration of faculty roles toward achieving a seamlessness between teaching, research, and service."

Boyer (1990) identified the scholarship of teaching as one of four types of scholarship—the others being the scholarship of discovery, the scholarship of integration, and the scholarship of application. The Carnegie Foundation for the Advancement of Teaching and the American Association for Higher Education (AAHE) have subsequently advanced this form of scholarship through work with faculty, campuses, and disciplinary associations (Cambridge, 2002; Hutchings & Shulman, 1999). While scholarly teaching, informed by deep understanding of one's field and how students learn in one's field, is a goal of many faculty, the scholarship of teaching and learning goes further to encourage teachers to study processes of teaching and learning and their outcomes. Barbara Cambridge (2001), vice president of AAHE, explains: "The scholarship of teaching and learning addresses the intellectual work of the classroom, especially teaching and learning, as the focus of disciplinary-based inquiry, captures that work in appropriate formats for self-reflection or presentation to peers, and applies the results to practice" (p. 5).

Since the early 1990s, campuses have used *teaching portfolios*—or *dossiers*, as they are called in Canada—to capture the scholarship of teaching. The notion of the teaching portfolio was introduced by the Canadian Association of University Teachers (Shore, Foster, Knapper, Nadeau, Neill, & Sim, 1986) and later adopted in the United States as well (Seldin, 2000, 2004). Some faculty developers consult with graduate students and faculty members who are developing teaching and course portfolios as a means of providing a fuller and more informative assessment of teaching for self-reflection, teaching awards, and personnel decision-making. McKinney (2004) suggests that those involved in faculty development can further promote the scholarship of teaching through small grant programs, institutes, or courses on doing and publishing scholarly work on teaching, helping to facilitate scholarship of teaching writing circles, and providing resources, such as books, journals, and web sites for faculty engaged in this work.

While all institutions identified the scholarship of teaching as an important topic, community colleges identified this issue as important to address through faculty development programming only to a moderate extent (mean: 2.83). Moreover, community colleges are currently providing fewer faculty development services in this area in comparison to other institutional types (mean: 2.07). The reason for this notable exception is not clear. It is apparent, however, that some respondents wanted to further the approach on their campuses. A community college assistant center director stated: "We need more focus on the scholarship of teaching—finding a solid way to investigate and change our teaching/learning paradigm." Two Hesburgh Award programs are built around this concept.

- *Indiana University–Bloomington, 2003 Hesburgh Award Winner.* The Scholarship of Teaching and Learning Program at Indiana University–Bloomington has encouraged faculty members to explore a variety of educational approaches and to reflect on questions about student learning derived from their experiences in the classroom. The broadest impact on learning came from a series of campus-wide colloquia, held throughout the academic year, on educational research and results. The sessions were led both by faculty members from Bloomington and by visitors from other campuses.

- *Alverno College, 1994 Hesburgh Award Winner.* Faculty at Alverno College needed support structures to adapt to a redesigned curriculum that included not only mastery of academic disciplines but also essential skills. Thus faculty had joint appointments in an "ability department" as well as a discipline. Ability departments relied on a team approach, and faculty developed a sense of ownership and responsibility for the curriculum. The academic calendar was restructured to provide time for faculty to meet regularly and exchange ideas at college institutes, regular department meetings, all-college workshops, and extensive orientations.

Writing across the curriculum/writing to learn

Rounding out the top tier of issues for which faculty developers felt it was important to provide services was writing across the curriculum/writing to learn (mean: 3.06). In an analysis conducted in the mid-1980s of a wide variety of faculty development activities at many different institutions, Eble and McKeachie (1985) found that writing across the curriculum workshops were among the most frequently offered faculty development services. These programs were also rated among the most effective by program directors. A decade later, interest in writing across the curriculum and writing to learn as part of faculty development programming continued (Cottell, Hansen, &

Ronald, 2000; Sorcinelli & Elbow, 1997; Walvoord, Hunt, Dowling, & McMahon, 1996). Caldwell and Sorcinelli (1997) reported that workshops and seminars that helped faculty improve student learning through writing were among the best attended and most highly rated events at their research university. They also suggested ways in which teaching development programs could form a partnership with writing programs to improve teaching and learning.

In contrast, the faculty development respondents in this study indicated that the importance of writing across the curriculum (mean: 3.06) was not matched by the extent of activities offered (mean: 2.46). Developers from liberal arts colleges saw writing across the curriculum as more important to offer (mean: 3.45) than their counterparts at research and doctoral universities, comprehensive universities, and community colleges. The data also indicate that liberal arts colleges are offering more faculty development programs on writing across the curriculum and writing to learn than any of the other institutional types (mean: 2.96). One comprehensive university that has offered an award-winning writing across the curriculum program is Robert Morris University.

- *Robert Morris University, 1998 Hesburgh Certificate of Excellence Winner.* The Writing Across the Curriculum Program has served as the heart of the faculty development program at Robert Morris University for more than a decade. Over 50% of faculty members have worked on programs that use writing to improve student communication and learning. The university has developed a two-phase approach to maintaining faculty training and interest. The program has produced more than a dozen interactive video conferences and resource tapes, and worked with partner institutions to integrate its program with their respective curricula.

Current Issues Least Addressed Through Faculty Development Services

Overall, faculty developers rated several issues as less than moderately important and typically offered to a slight extent or not at all. These issues included course and curriculum reform, course and teaching portfolios, teaching in online and distance environments (although programs on this topic were slightly more likely), peer review, mentoring faculty from underrepresented populations, the shifting characteristics and demographics of students, teaching underprepared students, community service-learning, teaching adult learners, general education, team teaching, graduate student teaching development, and post-tenure review.

Three issues deserve particular mention. Faculty developers across institutional types ranked the following three current issues as both least important for their programs to address and offered "not at all" or "to a slight extent" in their faculty development services.

Table 4.2: Mean Ratings of Issues Least Addressed as Important to Offer and Currently Offered

Issue	Important to Offer	Currently Offered
General education reform	2.60	1.98
Team teaching	2.49	1.91
Post-tenure review	2.33	1.62

General education reform

General education has been revitalized over the last two decades, and many higher education institutions have reviewed and revised their undergraduate curricula through campus task forces on general education, assessment projects on the core curriculum, and a range of curricular and faculty development initiatives (Gaff, 1991, 1999; Stark & Lattuca, 1996). Gaff (1999) found that such initiatives have resulted in more attention to fundamental intellectual skills, interdisciplinary study, the liberal arts, and the particular needs of first-year students. New ideas and trends include increased attention to the interrelation of general education and the major, to the teaching and learning process, and to global and domestic diversity.

Overall, however, faculty developers did not identify this topic as one for which they currently offered programming in any significant way, nor did they rate the issue as a particularly important focus for programming. Respondents from liberal arts colleges and community colleges considered general education reform to be somewhat more important to address through faculty development services than did respondents at other institutions; nevertheless, programming on this topic at these institutions was reported to occur only to a slight extent.

There are several possible explanations for this finding. First, general education reform is likely to fall under the domain of faculty leaders and administrators in academic affairs (e.g., program chair, dean, vice president) more often than in a faculty development office. Reform is also likely to be played out at a range of organizational levels—course, program, and institution—sometimes making it a challenge for faculty development programs to know how and at which level to enter the reform effort. Moreover, when the revival of interest in general education began, attention focused almost exclusively on content, with little notice given to strategies for teaching and learning.

Gaff (1999) suggests that more recent research on the undergraduate experience supports faculty and student development approaches such as learning communities, experiential and service learning, collaborative group projects, and attention to diversity-related issues. Cook (2001) argues that teaching centers can play a crucial role in curricular reform. For example, they can gather evaluation and assessment data about the current curriculum so that faculty decisions about improvements are based on empirical evidence, organize and facilitate meetings and retreats at which faculty make curricular decisions, and provide pedagogical expertise and resources to help with course design or redesign. We predict that faculty developers will be increasingly active in helping instructors and administrators incorporate these activities into general education programs. Several programs have already received Hesburgh Awards for such approaches to general education reform.

- *Barnard College, 2004 Hesburgh Award Winner.* The innovative program Reacting to the Past breathed new life into Barnard College's first-year, general education offerings. The program challenges students to debate the ideas and politics of great figures from the past, such as Socrates and Gandhi, through intense role-playing games. Students acquire considerable speaking skills and a heightened ability to empathize with other cultures and people.

- *University of Missouri–Columbia, 1997 Hesburgh Award Winner.* In order to deal with the narrow general education preparation of graduates and an unproductive system of electives, University of Missouri–Columbia developed a coherent framework of breadth and depth for the General Education Program consisting of seven components. The program fostered faculty collaboration and interdisciplinary linkages.

- *Seattle University, 1993 Hesburgh Certificate of Excellence Winner.* The Faculty Development Program for the New Core Curriculum at Seattle University consisted of seminars and workshops addressing major issues or problems within the new integrated, three-phase curriculum that replaced the previously fragmented core requirements.

Team teaching

Team teaching can take several forms, but most commonly involves two or more instructors teaching the same course. Faculty often regard team-taught courses as a creative way both to collaborate with colleagues and to offer interdisciplinary approaches to classroom learning (Davies, 1995; Robinson & Schaible, 1995; Smith & McCann, 2001). While team teaching is not the norm in most colleges, a few institutions, such as The Evergreen State College, are organized almost entirely around collaborative teaching and learning (Smith, 1994).

Overall, faculty developers did not offer many services to support this approach to classroom instruction, nor did they identify team teaching methods as critically important to address in their programs. Given that the goal of many faculty development programs is to foster collegiality and community, this finding may seem surprising. Yet team teaching opportunities often emerge from departmental or multidisciplinary initiatives, rather than at a campus-wide or system level. Barriers such as cost and lowered productivity in terms of student credit often stand in the way of development efforts in this area (Smith, 1994). It is useful, however, for administrators and faculty developers to ask who on campus is creating the structures that support team teaching and developing teachers who can team teach, particularly since faculty report that they value such collaborative efforts.

One notable example of a consortium that operates a statewide support system for collaborative teaching and highlights team teaching in their offerings has been recognized:

* *The Evergreen State College, 1994 Hesburgh Certificate of Excellence.* At the Washington Center for Improving the Quality of Undergraduate Education at The Evergreen State College, the key assumptions are that faculty development must be tied to curriculum improvement and assessment. The center has promoted learning communities as a holistic approach to curriculum reform, faculty development, and assessment

and has linked participating institutions through faculty exchange programs, team teaching, seed grants, consultants, and annual conferences.

Post-tenure review

Post-tenure review was the issue for which developers from all institutional types currently offered the fewest services and which they ranked as least important to address through their faculty development programs. Post-tenure review is a system of formal, periodic evaluation that is separate from the many traditional forms of ongoing evaluation used in most colleges and universities, such as annual faculty reports, reviews for reappointment, and course or teaching evaluations (Association of American Universities, 2001).

Over the last few years, several useful publications have chronicled how post-tenure review is being addressed, delineated perceived benefits and drawbacks, and offered case studies of model programs (Alstete, 2000; Aper & Fry, 2003; Licata & Morreale, 2002; O'Meara, 2003). The policies for post-tenure review vary widely in terms of purposes, audience, implementation, and outcomes. For example, purposes can focus on rewarding strong performance or addressing substandard performance. Review can apply to all faculty or be event-triggered by particularly positive or negative annual reviews. Some campuses have noted benefits of post-tenure review, such as improved faculty productivity and morale, while others have noted high costs in terms of faculty and staff time, money, and other institutional resources.

Of particular interest to faculty developers is the issue of how to harmonize the potential of post-tenure review for faculty development with the linkage of most programs to personnel decision-making. Svinicki (1998) suggests that faculty developers can help the administration design reasonable review systems that respect both the strengths of the faculty member and the needs of the institution for legitimate measures of effectiveness. Faculty development centers can also support faculty who ask for help as they go through the review process. The faculty development program at the University of

Massachusetts Amherst offers a model for how to work with faculty going through the post-tenure review process. It was designed in consultation with senior faculty, chairs, deans, and representatives of the faculty union. The Periodic Multi Year Review Grants for Professional Development in Teaching provide incentives for teaching improvements and individual consultation to set project goals and to assess outcomes (visit http://www.umass.edu/cft for more information). No Hesburgh Award recipients highlighted post-tenure review in their model programs.

Differences in Key Issues and Services by Institutional Type

Differences among types of institutions in the priority of issues and current programming tended to reflect the particular missions of those institutions. For example, preparing the future professoriate (mean: 3.45) and graduate student teaching development (mean: 3.29) were two services that research/doctoral faculty developers cited as important to offer. Indeed, at many research universities, programs such as Preparing Future Faculty, teaching assistant orientations, and courses on college teaching are increasingly available for graduate students through graduate schools, provosts' offices, offices of TA development, or teaching centers (Wulff & Austin, 2004).

   In contrast, comprehensive universities and liberal arts and community colleges did not see assisting graduate student teaching development as an important issue to address through faculty development services. Intuitively, these results make sense, since it is primarily within the research universities that doctoral students are studying and serving as TAs and where TAs are used to cover portions of the institutional teaching load. While some comprehensive institutions and liberal arts and community colleges collaborate with research universities through Preparing Future Faculty Programs, and all of these institutions are certainly interested in the quality of graduates who seek employment as teachers in their institutions, their attention to graduate education would likely be focused on departments rather than faculty development offices. Faculty developers at research/doctoral universities also listed offering services to support the development of course/teaching portfolios as more important than did respondents from other institutions.

Faculty developers at liberal arts colleges provided more programming on writing across the curriculum/writing to learn and rated its importance more highly than developers at other types of institutions (mean: 3.45). This higher rating may reflect the fact that faculty development programs at small liberal arts colleges often collaborate with faculty and students to advance students' abilities in written and oral communication skills. Moreover, developing higher-order thinking skills through first-year seminars and capstone courses involving intensive writing are long-standing curricular emphases at most liberal arts colleges.

The priorities of faculty developers in community colleges offered a sharp contrast to those in other institutional types. Overall, they rated more highly the importance of offering services pertaining to assessment of student learning (mean: 3.67), teaching underprepared students (mean: 3.44), teaching in online and distance environments (mean: 3.41), and teaching adult learners (mean: 3.32). They also reported offering services pertaining to these topics at a level closer to that at which they thought the issues should be addressed. Historically, community colleges have emphasized access for diverse and adult learners and responsiveness to community and business needs. Given the large number of adult students and those with developmental needs, the tradition of open access, the pressure to document student learning outcomes, and the demand for online learning on community college campuses, developers are likely targeting areas of particular importance to their faculty.

Differences by Time in the Profession

The patterns of responses of experienced faculty developers (those working in the profession 10 or more years) mirrored those of newcomers with regard to issues most important to address in faculty development services or programs. Experienced faculty developers, however, tended to rate the importance of all 21 topics somewhat more highly than their newer colleagues. One exception to this pattern concerns the importance of services related to teaching in online and distance environments. Individuals newer to the profession rated the importance of providing these services slightly higher than did experienced faculty developers. Another exception concerned activities related to writing across the curriculum and writing to learn. In this case also, individuals newer to the profession rated these topics as more important to address through programming than did their more experienced colleagues.

Faculty Developers' Views:
New Issues and Extent of Services

When offered a set of 17 new challenges and pressures on institutions that affect faculty work, developers rated only 5 of them as important to be addressed through faculty development to more than a moderate extent (mean greater than 3.0). While faculty developers perceived some need for attention to these issues, they reported that their institutions are offering relevant services and resources pertaining to each of these issues to only a slight extent. (See Table 4.3.)

Table 4.3: Mean Ratings of Issues Important to Address and Not Currently Offered to a Great Extent

Issue	Important to Offer	Currently Offered
Training and supporting part-time and adjunct faculty	3.26	2.11
Changing faculty roles and rewards	3.18	2.18
Departmental leadership and management	3.10	1.94
Balancing multiple faculty roles	3.08	2.12
Interdisciplinary collaborations	3.05	2.24

Overall, developers rated several other new issues listed on the survey as important to address through faculty development to less than a moderate extent (mean less than 3.0). These issues include: support of institutional change priorities, preparing the future professoriate, faculty roles in learning communities, ethical conduct of faculty work, program assessment and accreditation, unit and program evaluation, collaborative departmental work teams, commitment to civic life and the public good, outreach and service activities, community-based research, and faculty and departmental entrepreneurship. Developers also indicated that their institutions are offering services or resources pertaining to these issues only slightly or not at all.

The next chapter explores in more detail the challenges that developers perceive faculty and their institutions are facing. It suggests the areas to which they may turn their attention in coming years.

Conclusion

Faculty developers are currently addressing many of the issues they and other academic leaders believe are important to higher education institutions today. Respondents to our survey reported that it was important to offer and that they do offer some services on significant issues such as student-centered learning, new faculty development, teaching technologies, pedagogies of engagement (such as active learning), assessment of student learning outcomes, multiculturalism and diversity, the scholarship of teaching, and writing across the curriculum. Current topics faculty developers are not offering many services on, or do not see as centrally important to address, include general education reform, team teaching, and post-tenure review. When offered a list of possible new issues confronting faculty members, developers indicated only a few that they believed should be addressed through faculty development. Furthermore, they reported that institutional services and resources for faculty pertaining to these new challenges and pressures are fairly modest.

Chapter highlights

- Faculty development programs and services are responding to important, complex, and fast-paced changes in the teaching and learning environment.

- A gap exists between issues that faculty developers believe are most important to offer and the extent to which they do offer services in support of these issues.

- While there is some general consensus on what faculty developers identify as most and least important issues and services, institutional differences exist. Many of these differences, however, can be attributed to institutional mission (e.g., community colleges and adult learners, research universities and TAs).

5

Future Priorities for
Faculty Development

T he nature of faculty work is changing. Teaching must effectively address the needs of a changing and diverse student body. Faculty members are now asked to engage with the broader society and to find creative uses for technology in their research and teaching. Faculty appointments are also in flux, with many institutions shifting the balance away from tenure-stream faculty appointments to part-time and contract arrangements. Faculty face an array of challenges, and the possible priorities for faculty development in the next several years are quite diverse.

Looking to the Future

In this chapter, we discuss what faculty developers perceive as the pressing challenges and issues facing faculty members and institutions. What are the issues that faculty development programs, services, and resources will likely need to address in the next five or ten years? What future directions will be important to consider when institutions make decisions about faculty development support, personnel, services, resources, and evaluation? The data presented here are based on responses to questions that asked respondents to identify "the top three challenges facing faculty" and "the top three challenges facing your institution" in regard to faculty work. We highlight issues faculty developers might consider as they plan the future of their units.

Our intent, however, is not to suggest that faculty developers must address each issue discussed in this chapter. We recognize that developers already handle many responsibilities. Moreover, faculty development may not be the best arena in which to respond to each issue. At some institutions some of these issues may already be addressed by units other than the faculty development office. Individual institutions might have contextual elements that determine the relative importance of addressing certain challenges. What we are suggesting is that institutional leaders—including, of course, faculty developers—carefully consider the expectations facing faculty members and the challenges facing colleges and universities and ask where and how their institutions are providing appropriate professional development support.

To explore possible directions for faculty development in the coming years, we asked developers to identify the top three challenges facing faculty and the top three challenges facing the institution concerning faculty work. As noted in Chapter 4, developers were asked to select these challenges from a list of 21 "current issues" and 17 "new challenges and pressures" or to offer additional issues not listed. Tables B and C in Appendix 2 list all the current issues and new challenges and directions pertaining to faculty work and provide data, including means and standard deviations, concerning respondents' perceptions of the importance of offering the services and the extent to which programs or institutions currently address each item.

Whereas Chapter 4 centered on important issues currently being addressed through faculty development, this chapter focuses on suggested new directions and priorities for faculty development. It identifies and reflects on developers' assessment of top challenges facing faculty members as well as major faculty work issues facing institutions of higher education, with particular attention to differences by institutional type. In analyzing the data on top challenges, we discovered that challenges facing faculty and their institutions varied by type of institution. Table 5.1 provides data on the percentages of respondents by institutional type who assessed each issue as a top-three challenge concerning faculty work for faculty members, and Table 5.2 provides data on the percentages of respondents by institutional type who assessed each issue as a top-three challenge concerning faculty work facing their institution. Similarities existed among many of the challenges facing research/doctoral universities, comprehensive universities, and liberal arts colleges. Community colleges were strikingly different; their challenges were closely linked to their mission of access and student success. This chapter also draws on the data from respondents' assessments of the extent to which such challenges are "currently addressed" through resources and services and "should be addressed" through faculty development. As in Chapter 4, we include Hesburgh award-winning faculty development programs that have been responsive to these key challenges.

Table 5.1: Faculty Challenges: Percentage of Developers Indicating the Issue Was One of the Top Three Challenges Facing Faculty

Challenge	Total	R/D	Comp	LA	CC
Balancing multiple roles	36.7	40.0	40.9	42.1	12.8
Changing faculty roles	32.3	35.2	34.0	33.9	12.8
Student-centered teaching	24.3	22.8	23.4	19.1	28.2
Teaching underprepared students	13.6	9.0	11.7	14.9	35.9
Assessing student-centered learning	24.2	24.9	21.3	29.5	35.9
Integrating technology	31.3	33.9	30.2	35.9	18.0
Training part-time/adjunct faculty	10.1	5.3	11.8	4.2	35.9
Departmental leadership/management	11.4	14.5	10.7	10.6	5.1

R/D = Research/Doctoral; Comp = Comprehensive; LA = Liberal Arts;
CC = Community College

Table 5.2: Institutional Challenges: Percentage of Developers Indicating the Issue Was One of the Top Three Challenges Facing Their Institution

Challenge	Total	R/D	Comp	LA	CC
Balancing multiple roles	20.0	24.2	19.1	26.0	5.3
Changing faculty roles	28.8	32.9	29.0	36.9	10.5
Student-centered teaching	12.2	12.6	6.1	10.9	20.9
Teaching underprepared students	9.2	3.8	11.0	10.7	25.9
Assessing student-centered learning	20.7	19.6	20.0	36.9	28.8
Integrating technology	18.5	20.7	17.1	13.0	5.3
Training part-time/adjunct faculty	13.6	5.0	21.0	4.3	49.3
Departmental leadership/management	27.3	28.0	29.9	19.6	28.8

R/D = Research/Doctoral; Comp = Comprehensive; LA = Liberal Arts;
CC = Community College

Top Challenges

What do developers see as the top issues facing faculty members and their institutions? What are the issues around which faculty members are likely to need support over the next several years? From the responses of developers to the wide range of issues, challenges, and pressures presented, five broad categories emerged:

- *Faculty roles:* Balancing multiple roles and learning new roles
- *Student learning:* Teaching for student-centered learning, assessing student outcomes, and teaching underprepared students
- *Technology:* Integrating technology strategically into teaching and learning environments

- *Part-time faculty:* Training and supporting part-time and adjunct faculty
- *Departmental leadership and management:* Increasing effectiveness in the institution by working with department chairs and establishing interdisciplinary collaborations

Faculty Roles

The topic of faculty roles and rewards has many facets, as is evidenced by the numerous conference sessions scheduled over the decade of forums on faculty roles and rewards hosted by the American Association of Higher Education (AAHE). These forums investigated new definitions of faculty work and workloads and explored applications of Boyer's (1990) four scholarships (teaching and learning, engagement, integration, and discovery) for campus policy and practice. They also searched for new ways to structure notions of rewards within institutional goals and priorities (Rice & Sorcinelli, 2002).

Two aspects of faculty roles and rewards were of particular concern to faculty developers at all types of institutions when they considered top challenges concerning faculty work:

- Balancing multiple roles
- Changing faculty roles

Balancing multiple roles

About 40% of the faculty developers at research universities, comprehensive institutions, and liberal arts colleges cited "faculty work balance" as one of the top three challenges facing faculty. The issue of balance is one that resonates across career stages. The literature on early-career faculty and graduate students aspiring to be faculty consistently highlights concerns about balance in their lives. In an environment in which professors are frequently criticized for not working hard enough, the greatest complaint voiced by new faculty is lack of time—being overwhelmed by multiple responsibilities. Newcomers struggle to prioritize teaching, research, and service responsibilities, as well as tasks they are often less trained for, such as student advising, grant-getting, and administrative duties. They also express concern about carving out time for family, leisure, and civic activities. New faculty often describe this phenomenon as an "overloaded plate" (Austin, 2002a; Menges & Associates, 1999; Rice, Sorcinelli, & Austin, 2000).

Experienced faculty members, too, find themselves pulled in many directions. While they are no longer driven by the tenure race, not having "enough time to do my work" is still a top complaint (Finkelstein & LaCelle-Peterson, 1993). Mid-career and senior faculty may be called upon to teach more, to act as mentors for graduate teaching assistants and new faculty, and to take on new administrative roles as others retire (Bland & Bergquist, 1997). It is no surprise, then, that department chairs, deans, and provosts increasingly see the need to pay attention to faculty priorities, the structure of the academic career, and the reward system (Diamond & Adam, 1995, 2000; Driscoll & Lynton, 1999; Wergin & Swingen, 2000).

The faculty developers we surveyed were keenly aware of the need to anticipate and respond to serious questions about how to balance faculty roles. A center director in a research university called for a renewed commitment to helping faculty achieve a sense of wholeness and integration in their work: "Faculty development needs to move to a community-based model. The traditional view of workshops, conferences, sabbaticals are still valuable, yet contribute to the sense of isolation on campuses. Faculty development needs to go back to its roots of addressing the 'whole person' rather than the current fragmented approach."

At comprehensive institutions, faculty members are especially likely to encounter the expectation that they will increase their research productivity while maintaining high teaching loads. This inflation of research expectations has contributed to what Ward and Wolf-Wendel (2003) describe as the rise of the "striving" comprehensive institution. They define these institutions as seeking to adopt research cultures like those of research universities, often while maintaining considerable teaching and service obligations. A comprehensive university center director recommended that institutions find ways to make the academic workplace more appealing: "We should be working toward humanizing higher education and making it an attractive place for our best and brightest to work and grow. I worry about the future of higher education—who will want to be faculty with so many professional pressures to publish, get tenure, get grants, etc.? Faculty quality of life is declining dramatically."

An interesting finding is that faculty developers from community colleges did not indicate balancing multiple roles as a top challenge in their institutional environment; only 13% of community college developers listed this as one of the top three challenges facing faculty, and only 5% listed it as one of the top three challenges facing their institutions. The responsibilities of community college faculty members often focus specifically on teaching and working with students. In fact, many two-year college faculty are part-time and are hired specifically to teach. Thus they feel less need to balance roles than faculty members in institutional types where the faculty role involves an expanded array of responsibilities, such as research, public service, institutional citizenship, and entrepreneurship.

Regardless of institutional type, respondents indicated that helping faculty find the appropriate balance among multiple roles is a responsibility faculty development programs should address (mean: 3.08). However, they indicated that their institutions were only addressing this challenge to a slight extent (mean: 2.12).

The issue of balance invites thoughtful attention by faculty developers and other institutional leaders. Several Hesburgh award programs also highlight approaches that are particularly relevant to balancing roles.

- *University of New Hampshire, 2002 Hesburgh Certificate of Excellence Winner.* The University of New Hampshire's Academic Program in College Teaching, based on a collaboration between the university's graduate school and its Teaching Excellence Program, was designed to prepare doctoral students for the rigors of college-level academic careers. Graduate students learned to analyze their teaching and learning outcomes. Faculty mentoring was focused on enhancing teaching effectiveness, but also expanded the readiness of doctoral candidates for scholarly and service responsibilities.

- *University of Massachusetts Amherst, 2000 Hesburgh Certificate of Excellence Winner.* The Center for Teaching at the University of Massachusetts Amherst has encouraged a culture that fosters interdisciplinary communities of teaching and learning both at and across the different stages of a faculty career—teaching assistant, pre-tenure faculty, mid-career, and senior faculty. Through a number of yearlong intensive programs, teaching fellows at different career stages receive support across their multiple faculty roles in a collaborative model of faculty development.

- *Miami-Dade Community College, 1993 Hesburgh Award Winner.* In response to the increasing numbers of nontraditional students as well as new faculty at Miami-Dade Community College, the college developed the faculty support and development Teaching/Learning Project to encompass all phases of the typical faculty member's career, including search committee training, extensive orientation for new faculty, two graduate courses in classroom research techniques and effective teaching styles, a college-wide student-feedback program, and a set of policies and procedures that govern tenure and promotion.

Changing faculty roles

About one-third (32%) of the faculty developers from research/doctoral universities, comprehensive universities, and liberal arts colleges identified "changing faculty roles," a concern related to balancing faculty roles, as one of their choices for the top three challenges facing faculty members and their institutions.

As the external context influencing higher education changes, so does the conception of faculty work, and new understandings are emerging of what it means to be a faculty member (Austin, 2002b; Rice, 1996). For example, some faculty roles now require expertise for which many faculty were not explicitly prepared. Faculty members at most institutional types are now expected to use technology in their teaching, conduct ongoing assessment of student learning, understand and meet the needs of a diverse group of students, and provide them with out-of-class support. At some institutions, faculty may also be encouraged to extend their teaching and scholarship by reaching out to local, national, and international constituencies (Driscoll & Lynton, 1999; Lynton, 1995). A faculty development center director at a liberal arts college commented on the complexity of faculty work and its implications for faculty *and* student development: "The field of faculty development should move in the direction of understanding and supporting the complex roles that faculty play as citizens of colleges and universities, as leaders of their institutions, as intellectuals in the larger world, and as role models for the educated men and women they hope to develop in turn." A developer from a research university pointed to the impact of technology: "We should especially pay attention to the changing role of faculty as universities embrace change, including teaching with technology and extending the academic community to communities outside university environments."

When we looked more closely at the composition of responses regarding the impact of changing faculty roles by institutional type, however, we found that only 13% of community college faculty developers indicated that changing faculty roles was one of the top three challenges facing their faculty, compared to the overall response level of 32%. Moreover, respondents from community colleges were least likely to rate this issue as important (mean: 2.90). The demand-response nature of community colleges (Gumport, 2003) creates an environment of constant change. Perhaps many of the trends associated with changing roles—replacement of full-time faculty with part-timers, the rise of accountability, the increased pressures for productivity—have already occurred at community colleges. Thus developers may not see addressing the issue of role change as necessary or even possible. And, as we mentioned earlier, faculty members in community colleges often focus specifically on teaching and working with students and may not feel great pressure to add new or different responsibilities.

Despite the challenges associated with changing faculty roles, developers believed overall that this challenge should be addressed through faculty development services (mean: 3.18). Yet respondents indicated that their institutions were only offering pertinent services or resources to a slight extent (mean: 2.12). Can professional developers and other academic leaders address this issue in a meaningful way? Seeking ways to help faculty members handle changing roles may be one of the areas where faculty development should consider expanding. Perhaps developers, along with faculty committees, department chairs, and deans, can help envision new strategies for helping faculty members handle the diverse responsibilities they are asked to fulfill.

Some members of the Professional and Organizational Development Network in Higher Education (POD Network) have worked with educational associations that have taken a lead in providing resources on balancing and changing faculty roles. For example, AAHE offered a series of working papers on faculty roles and rewards. The Council of Independent Colleges (CIC) conducted a two-year grant program that investigated new definitions of faculty roles and rewards in the context of institutional mission. The program concluded with a report that reconsiders faculty roles and rewards and presents promising practices for institutional change efforts (Zahorski & Cognard, 1999). EDUCAUSE offers targeted resources on the topic of where new technologies fit into traditional faculty roles and rewards (Hagner, Samson, & Starrett, 2003). Campus Compact, a national coalition of college and university presidents committed to civic education, has challenged faculty developers to include issues of community service-learning and community-university partnerships for responsible citizenship in their plans (Ehrlich,

2001; Kecskes, Spring, & Lieberman, 2004). Several Hesburgh awardees also focus on changing faculty roles.

- *Portland State University, 2002 Hesburgh Certificate of Excellence Winner.* Practicing their university's motto, "Let knowledge serve the city," Portland State University (PSU) students and faculty became involved in research and community-based learning with a broad spectrum of local business, education, and civic partners. The Community-University Partnership Program moved beyond service to campus-wide engagement with the Portland metropolitan community, across all aspects of the PSU curriculum.

- *Missouri Southern State College, 2001 Hesburgh Certificate of Excellence Winner.* A new international mission at Missouri Southern State College, Bringing the World to the Midwest, sought to bridge the gap between the local community and the global economy. An institutional study-abroad grant enabled the majority of full-time teaching faculty to immerse themselves in a foreign culture and to translate these experiences to the direct benefit of students in the classroom. Each year approximately one-fourth of the faculty receive funds for international travel. The college also instituted a sizable grant program for students to pursue study abroad.

- *Prince George's Community College, 1997 Hesburgh Certificate of Excellence Winner.* The Science and Technology Resource Center at Prince George's Community College was designed to improve science and technology instruction and learning and fostered a range of innovative professional development programs. In-service programs for K–12 included workshops, institutes for specific disciplines, semester-long courses, and mentoring activities. Many of the professional development programs have resulted in partnerships with colleges and universities, government agencies, local schools, and private industry.

Student Learning Issues

A number of developers identified the following issues pertaining to student learning among the top challenges concerning faculty work.

- Teaching for student-centered learning
- Assessing student learning outcomes
- Teaching underprepared students

We include teaching underprepared students in this section because developers at community colleges rated it highly; 36% of these developers listed it among the top challenges concerning faculty work.

Teaching for student-centered learning

Faculty developers see the need to engage in student-centered learning as a continuing challenge for faculty members. Twenty-four percent of all faculty developers in this study identified this issue as one of the top three challenges confronting faculty. As discussed in Chapter 4, there is a rich and growing research literature that supports student-centered learning, learning that focuses on the student and on the kind of teaching that will support desired learning. This topic incorporates and transcends many of the issues we have discussed, including changing faculty roles, active and collaborative learning, diversity, technology, and assessment.

Overall, developers identified teaching for student-centered learning as one of the top three challenges that can be addressed through faculty development (28%). What differs here from some of the other challenges that confront faculty is that developers reported that their institutions are already providing substantial support and resources to help faculty teach with a student-centered learning focus (mean: 3.25). Indeed, as noted in Chapter 4, many faculty development programs are already in place to offer training and support to help faculty members teach in ways that are focused on enhancing student learning.

But teaching for student learning also requires finding out how much learning is actually taking place. This question is one that is increasingly asked of faculty members and institutions in serious and sustained ways, as is suggested in the following discussion of assessment. The importance of this question, as well as the kind of complex skills required of teachers to effectively enable and evaluate student-centered learning, is reflected in the fact that, overall, developers selected this issue as both most important to address and as one of the top three challenges faculty will face in the future.

See Chapter 4 for a more complete discussion of this topic and for descriptions of several Hesburgh Award programs that emphasize teaching for student-centered learning.

Assessing student learning outcomes

Overall, 24% of developers identified assessing student learning outcomes as one of the top three challenges facing their faculty, and 21% listed it as one of the top three challenges facing their institutions. In Chapter 4 we noted the growing demand for assessment of student learning outcomes, the range of faculty development services now offered, and faculty developers' concern about an overemphasis on assessment for accountability rather than for improvement in teaching and learning.

The need for colleges and universities to take responsibility for assessing student learning is unambiguous. But the need for balance and more integration between assessment used for improvement of teaching and learning and for accountability is also apparent to faculty developers. While balancing multiple roles, changing faculty roles, and teaching for student-centered learning were cited more often as faculty challenges than as institutional challenges, assessment of student learning was viewed within all institutional types as a critical issue for institutions as well as for faculty.

The issue of assessing student learning was identified as one of the top three challenges confronting faculty by approximately a third of community college (36%) and liberal arts college (30%) respondents. Developers at both institutional types also cited assessment as one of the top three challenges facing their institutions, with 29% of community college and 37% of liberal arts college developers agreeing. The issue was somewhat less critical to developers from comprehensive and research universities. Twenty-one percent of the developers from comprehensive institutions listed assessing student learning as a top challenge for faculty members, as did 25% of those at research universities. A fifth (20%) of comprehensive and research university developers indicated that assessment of student learning outcomes was a top institutional issue.

Assessing student learning is not only perceived as an important challenge, but it is also one of the top three challenges that developers believe can and should be addressed through faculty development. Faculty development has long seen assessment as a powerful tool for diagnosing and improving student learning at the course- or program-based level. But agencies at the state and federal levels and accrediting associations are increasingly demanding assurance of learning at the institutional level. Suggestions of policies to improve the quality of learning include mandatory participation in student assessment surveys and public reporting of results, establishing competitive grants for teaching, and improving accreditation (Newman, Couturier, & Scurry, 2004). The POD Network has recently begun initiating discussions and offering sessions on the linkages between the work of teaching and learning centers and institutional accrediting agencies such as the Middle States Association of Colleges and Schools and the New England Association of Schools and Colleges.

Despite these efforts, it appears that faculty development programs cannot accommodate the demand for such services and resources. Although developers placed a high importance on providing support in this area (mean: 3.43), they assessed current offerings of services more modestly (mean: 2.57).

See Chapter 4 for literature on this topic and descriptions of several Hesburgh Award programs that focus on the assessment of student learning.

Teaching underprepared students

For faculty developers in community colleges, teaching underprepared students is one of the top three challenges facing their faculty and institutions. A core mission of community colleges is to provide open access to educational opportunities for students and community members. This policy often means that upwards of 40% of entering students require remediation in various academic skills (Cohen & Brawer, 2003). Indeed, according to Alexander Astin (2004), "The education of the remedial student is the most important educational problem in America today, more important than educational funding, affirmative action, vouchers, merit pay, teacher education, financial aid, curriculum reform and the rest" (p. 1).

Faculty developers at community colleges are attuned to the importance of teaching the underprepared student. Thirty-six percent of these developers identified the issue of teaching underprepared students as a top challenge for faculty, and 26% listed it as a top challenge for their institutions. However, community college faculty development centers are not providing services (mean: 2.73) at a level that matches the perceived importance of the issue (mean: 3.44). The responsibility for underprepared students may more often fall to academic staff in a student learning center rather than to a faculty development program or academic department. This raises the question of how faculty development and other offices might address the needs of such students more broadly and deeply across the curriculum.

Most higher education institutions have some programs or strategies to help underprepared students learn, but such programs are most often found in community colleges. Not surprisingly, faculty developers from liberal arts, comprehensive, and research institutions did not include this issue as one of the top three challenges they saw confronting their faculty, nor did they rate this issue very highly in terms of the importance of offering faculty development services and resources.

Astin (2004) argues that rather than see the underprepared student as a burden or a threat to institutional excellence, we need to understand that we and our society have an enormous stake in what happens to these students and that their needs should be addressed more broadly throughout higher education. Thus it was encouraging to discover that research and comprehensive universities and liberal arts colleges are offering exemplary programs to support underprepared students, as is suggested by the following Hesburgh Award programs.

- *Indiana University–Purdue University Indianapolis, 2002 Hesburgh Certificate of Excellence Winner.* The Gateway Program to Enhance Student Retention at Indiana University–Purdue University Indianapolis collaboratively joined a faculty development effort with a student support effort to improve student success and retention. The program emphasized grassroots participation across campus and fostered dialogue among the faculty.

- *University of Nebraska–Omaha, 2001 Hesburgh Certificate of Excellence Winner.* At the University of Nebraska–Omaha, the Goodrich Scholarship Program has focused on the retention of underrepresented students who, once recruited, are at a greater risk of failure. The faculty development component included monthly meetings, faculty acting as resources within departments and helping to develop programs such as Women's Studies, and a national focus through workshops and conference presentations relating to the Goodrich Scholarship Program.

- *Brooklyn College of the City University of New York, 1998 Hesburgh Certificate of Excellence Winner.* Brooklyn College of the City University of New York designed TRANSFORMATIONS, a multifaceted faculty development program that played a pivotal role in strengthening the academic and support programs for first-year students in the Freshman Year College, to promote the retention of students, to build faculty dialogue and awareness, and to develop established connections between courses.

| Integrating Technology into Teaching and Learning

Chapter 4 shows that developers rated the importance of offering services and support for integrating technology into traditional teaching and learning settings quite highly. Thirty-one percent of all respondents indicated that the integration of technology into traditional teaching was one of the top three challenges facing faculty members (mean: 3.51).

Due to rapid technological advances, faculty members are called on to provide responsive, low-cost education opportunities and to develop educational delivery in new formats—through web sites, short modules, and certificate programs. Many faculty members have not been trained to teach in these new contexts. While specific needs vary because of differing levels of experience and interest, teachers require support and training to function optimally in such a rapidly changing technological environment (Baldwin, 1998).

Thirty-six percent of those surveyed from liberal arts colleges indicated that integrating technology into teaching and learning settings is a top challenge confronting faculty, as did 34% of the respondents from research/doctoral universities, and 30% of those from comprehensive institutions. In contrast, 36% of developers in community colleges indicated that offering and teaching online courses was a critical challenge for their faculty, while only 18% identified integrating technology into traditional teaching and learning settings as one of the top three challenges facing their faculty.

As the field of faculty development moves forward, developers in this study recognized that technology in the classroom—traditional or virtual—is a challenge that can be addressed through faculty development (33%). It is already being addressed in many institutions' faculty development programs (see Chapter 4), although the need for services, resources, and training is likely far from saturated. As noted in Chapter 2, the small percentage of faculty developers who identified themselves as technology coordinators raises the question of how faculty development programs will continue to incorporate technological issues into their concerns about teaching and learning. Despite this challenge, faculty developers do see that supporting faculty as they learn about and integrate technology into their teaching will continue to be an important part of an institution's faculty development plan. They recognize that digital technology will continue to change not only how teachers teach and students learn, but also how institutions will conduct their fundamental teaching and research missions. See Chapter 4 for literature on this topic and related Hesburgh Award programs.

Training and Supporting Part-Time and Adjunct Faculty

Overall, developers believe that addressing the needs of part-time and adjunct faculty is one of the most important new directions for faculty development (mean: 3.26). However, this issue only surfaces among developers in community colleges as one of three top challenges facing faculty and their institutions.

Although considerable debate surrounds the increasing use of part-time faculty and the decline of full-time tenure-stream positions, it is a distinctive trend that merits serious attention (Baldwin & Chronister, 2001; Finkelstein, Seal, & Schuster, 1998b; Finkelstein & Schuster, 2001; Gappa & Leslie, 1993, 1997). Finkelstein and Schuster (2001) cite data indicating that about one-half of the current faculty members in the United States are part-time and that "the majority of all full-time faculty appointments made in the 1990s . . . were off the tenure track" (p. 5). Appointing part-time or adjunct faculty enables institutions to maintain flexibility as students' academic interests shift, to hire talented professionals who are interested in sharing lessons from their work experience with students, and to minimize the financial commitments associated with full-time positions. Although some part-timers hope to secure full-time appointments eventually, others have a variety of reasons for choosing part-time positions—other professional work, family or home responsibilities, a desire to balance faculty work with other interests.

Whether they have chosen a part-time position or not, however, part-time faculty members face a number of challenges. Often, they are not included in regular faculty meetings and have little chance to exchange information with colleagues. They might not have offices for meeting with students or access to phones, and they might not be invited to faculty development opportunities or provided with funds for professional travel.

As noted, the perception that the needs of part-time and adjunct faculty are important to address appears to be greatest in community colleges (mean: 3.71) and comprehensive universities (mean: 3.37), probably because these types of institutions are particularly likely to employ part-time faculty. At research and doctoral institutions, graduate students fill many teaching needs (although there are reports of an increasing use of part-time faculty on these campuses as well). Four- and two-year undergraduate institutions, however, do not have graduate students to carry part of the teaching load. In fact, community colleges may hire up to 60% of their teaching staff on an adjunct basis (Cohen & Brawer, 2003). Not surprisingly, therefore, faculty development professionals at community colleges are particularly attentive to the importance of providing training and support for part-time and adjunct faculty. In fact, 50% of the survey respondents from community colleges (the greatest percentage across all institutional types) indicated that training and supporting part-time and adjunct faculty is among the top three challenges for their institutions, with 36% indicating it as a top challenge for faculty as well.

One community college developer argued that faculty development should be a budgeted component of institutional planning efforts, but also realized that professional development budgets would be strained by the needs of large numbers of part-time faculty: "Healthy institutions should be searching for ways to integrate faculty development into normal, ongoing expectations for all faculty and allocating 5% to 10% to ongoing support and training. Unfortunately, the increasing use of part-time faculty will create enormous and increasing stress on institutional budget priorities . . . especially in community colleges."

Twenty-one percent of the developers at comprehensive institutions indicated that training and supporting part-time and adjunct faculty was one of the top institutional challenges concerning faculty work. Although only a very small percentage of developers in liberal arts colleges, doctoral institutions, and research universities identified this as a top challenge for their faculty or their institutions, they did indicate that attention to faculty development support and services for part-time and adjunct faculty was important to offer (total mean: 3.26). In written comments, a faculty development center director in a liberal arts college suggested that "the lack of teaching/learning support of adjuncts for first year and second year students leads to fragmentation." A research university center director joined the chorus for "moving toward support for part-time faculty adjuncts."

A growing number of institutions are constructing faculty development programs and providing resources aimed at making part-time and adjunct faculty part of the academic community (Krupar, 2004; Lyons, 2003). Features of such programs include orientations, classroom management coaching and tools, technology enhancement training, team building and professional development opportunities, and peer-based as well as student-based evaluations of teaching. Krupar argues that such programs can greatly assist adjunct faculty in creating curriculum, advising students, facilitating student learning, and building community. Several Hesburgh Award programs have also addressed this issue.

- *Metropolitan State College of Denver, 2001 Hesburgh Certificate of Excellence Winner.* Metropolitan State College of Denver developed Bringing Adjuncts in from the Cold, a program of training, internships, and workshops addressing issues of instructional excellence, enhancing technology skills, improving adjunct advising, mentoring, and classroom management skills for the college's large population of adjunct instructors.

- *College of the Canyons, 1999 Hesburgh Certificate of Excellence Winner.* The Associate Program at College of the Canyons, a series of six weekend workshops based on microteaching, accommodated the needs of part-time faculty, offered practical professional development experiences relating to the classroom, and provided the opportunity to develop new connections to other people and places on campus. Other components of the program included in-depth discussions of innovative teaching techniques and mentor relationships.

- *Metropolitan State University, 1995 Hesburgh Certificate of Excellence Winner.* The Faculty Professional Development Program and the Teaching Center Committee at Metropolitan State University met the needs of adjunct faculty with flexible session times for workshops, multicultural education programs, and quarterly new faculty orientations. Each of the resident faculty oversaw 15–25 part-time faculty members. In addition, the program sponsored a lunchtime series, faculty mentoring programs, six-week teaching seminars, and teaching development grants.

Departmental Leadership and Management

Arguably, the preparation, training, and ongoing support of department leaders and other administrators are a critical and strategic institutional investment. Indeed, almost one-quarter of the respondents from research universities, comprehensive institutions, and community colleges identified the training and support of department chairs and heads as one of the top three institutional challenges. Developers also rated the need to provide training for departmental leadership and management as moderately high (mean: 3.10) when asked to indicate whether faculty development attention should be directed to this issue. Helping to develop interdisciplinary collaborations, though not identified as a top challenge, was indicated as an important new direction (mean: 3.10). Collaborations between departments and programs are generally facilitated by strong departmental leadership.

Working with department chairs

Over one-quarter (27%) of faculty developers indicated that support of departmental leadership was one of the top three challenges facing their institutions, and it was deemed a significant challenge by developers at all types of institutions.

Since the department is the locus for a great deal of the work of a university or college, department chairs and heads hold significant positions within the institution. They must be able to facilitate faculty work, support morale, administer departmental business, and serve as a bridge between senior institutional leaders and individual faculty members. They are responsible for interpreting administrators' decisions and helping deans and provosts understand the concerns of individual faculty members. Often chairs or heads strive to maintain their own research and teaching interests while also leading their units and managing an array of administrative details. Budget constraints, common in recent years at many institutions, have heightened expectations for chairs and heads to be effective as budget managers and entrepreneurs. The ability to frame a vision and inspire commitment, energy, and creativity is also part of the repertoire of an effective department head or chair (Lucas, 1994, 2002; Wolverton, Gmelch, & Sorenson, 1998). Because departments are the organizational units that link the faculty member and the university or college, chairs must consider and connect both the interests of the department and the institution. It is a demanding position, often having ambiguous demands (Lucas, 1994; Hecht, Higgerson, Gmelch, & Tucker, 1999; Pew Higher Education Roundtable, 1996; Wolverton, Gmelch, & Sorenson, 1998).

At some universities and colleges, the retirement of longtime leaders means that others must step into their roles. For example, a faculty development center director at a liberal arts college noted concerns about "the lack of leadership once baby boomers retire." Retirements, however, are not the only issue. As administrative hierarchies become flatter (Green 1990; Peterson & Dill, 1997), department chairs must assume more responsibility (Lucas, 2002). Historically, chairs have come from the faculty. Often they are well-regarded scholars, but they may not have had any particular preparation for the leadership and managerial responsibilities they face. Recognizing that the role of chair or head is a very demanding—and sometimes thankless—task, and that the effectiveness of department leaders contributes directly to the work of the institution, some universities and colleges are providing in-house professional development and training for their department chairs and heads, as well as opportunities for collegial interaction with others in the role. Overall, faculty developers indicated that the issue merits more institutional attention.

Members of the POD Network have offered a range of strategies for faculty developers to work collaboratively with department chairs (Hecht, 2001; Lucas, 2002). These include assisting chairs with setting tasks within the context of departmental and institutional goals, managing time and tasks, and managing relationships with colleagues and other academic leaders in the institution.

Beyond individual universities and colleges, a number of associations and other organizations have turned their attention to the challenges facing chairs. For example, the American Council on Education hosts regional workshops and a Department Chair Online Resource Center, which contains articles, practical suggestions, bibliographies, and links to other sites. The IDEA Center at Kansas State University offers an annual conference as well as a feedback system designed for college department chairs. Among professional associations, the American Political Science Association offers an e-handbook for political science department chairs as well as a conference for chairs as part of their annual meeting. Topics have included professional preparation and placement, distance learning, and post-tenure review. There are several handbooks that provide practical guidance for those managing academic departments (Gmelch & Miskin, 2004; Leaming, 1998; Lucas & Associates, 2000). Another resource is *The Department Chair,* a quarterly periodical that offers information and advice, often from a hands-on perspective.

Interdisciplinary collaborations

Issues previously discussed were identified by substantial percentages of respondents as among the top three challenges facing faculty or the top three challenges concerning faculty work facing their institutions. While only 2.8% of faculty developers identified interdisciplinary collaboration as a top-three challenge for faculty (5% being the largest percentage of developers across all institutional types indicating that this was a top-three challenge for faculty or their institutions), interdisciplinary collaborative efforts were seen as at least moderately important to address via faculty development programs (mean: 3.05). We include it here because, while developers did not explicitly identify this as one of the top challenges, they did rate it fairly high on our survey list of possible new directions that should be addressed through faculty development.

Interdisciplinary collaboration can mean teaching a course with multiple departments involved, offering joint degree programs, or working on research projects from a multidisciplinary perspective. It can also mean the kind of interdisciplinary teaching communities first established at research-intensive universities through the Lilly Teaching Fellows Program, and expanded to include faculty learning communities at institutions of all sizes and types (Cox & Richlin, 2004). Respondents seemed to be interested in a variety of types of collaboration, ranging from interdisciplinary programs to incorporating service-learning into academic experiences. For example, a research university center director called for "a focus on building interdisciplinary teams and programs, integrating technology, and linking service-learning in the community."

Despite the fact that developers consider interdisciplinary work to be an area important to address through faculty development services and resources, developers across institutional types indicated that this topic is not currently addressed much through faculty development (mean: 2.24). Interdisciplinary work is usually the result of individual faculty members deciding to engage in team teaching across departments or pursuing new areas in the course of their research. Hence this issue may not have gained the attention of faculty developers or other institutional leaders as one requiring explicit support and attention, with the notable exception of the Lilly Teaching Fellows model. With growing interest in supporting interdisciplinary education through such agencies as the National Science Foundation, this topic seems worthy of greater attention as a focus for faculty development. Exemplary Hesburgh Award programs provide varied and useful models for interdisciplinary programs.

- *Miami University of Ohio, 2003 Hesburgh Certificate of Excellence Winner.* Miami University of Ohio's Faculty Learning Communities (FLC) are yearlong intensive communities. Cohort-based FLCs include communities for junior faculty, senior faculty, department chairs, and graduate students. Topic-based FLCs have focused on issues such as team teaching, problem-based learning, diversity, ethics, and teaching writing-intensive courses. Major outcomes include departmental teaching evaluation plans, rewards for excellent teaching based on teaching portfolios, and faculty engagement in new teaching approaches.

- *The Evergreen State College, 1994 Hesburgh Certificate of Excellence Winner.* The Washington Center for Improving the Quality of Undergraduate Education at The Evergreen State College was designed as a statewide initiative to meet two needs in higher education: building an academic community within and among institutions and bringing faculty and administrators together to improve undergraduate education. The center provides a structure for programs such as faculty exchange, interdisciplinary and team teaching, seed grants, consultants, annual conferences, and several publications related to teaching.

• *New York University, 1993 Hesburgh Certificate of Excellence Winner.* At New York University (NYU) the Faculty Resource Network linked NYU faculty with faculty from liberal arts colleges in the New York area and Historically Black Colleges in the South to counter the isolation that faculty members at small colleges may feel. Programs included the Scholar-in-Residence Program that brought faculty to NYU to work on teaching or research projects, the University Associates Program for those within commuting distance of New York, and the Visiting Scholars Exchange Program to share ideas. Conferences, summer seminars, workshops, and institutes were also sponsored yearly.

New Directions Not Emphasized by Developers

Faculty developers indicated that several challenges proposed in the survey as possible new directions should be addressed by faculty development somewhat less than the issues just discussed. These include support of institutional change priorities, preparing the future professoriate, faculty roles in learning communities, ethical conduct of faculty work, program assessment (accreditation), unit and program evaluation, commitment to civic life and the public good, collaborative department work teams, post-tenure review, outreach and service activities, community-based research, and entrepreneurship (see mean values for each in Appendix 2, Table B).

A variety of factors may account for the lack of overall interest in addressing these challenges through faculty development. Institutional difference may be key here. For example, preparing the future professoriate is an important challenge for developers at research and doctoral institutions, but not at other institutional types. Other areas of institutions may offer programming and support. Indeed, this reason was suggested by a number of respondents in open-ended comments. In some cases, institutional context factors make these issues less relevant. Many of these challenges not emphasized by developers address faculty roles beyond teaching, and, as discussed in previous chapters, teaching and student learning issues still predominate the priorities and current services of faculty development programs.

Developers are particularly hesitant to expand upon their portfolio of responsibilities by adding new domains outside of the areas that have traditionally been addressed by faculty development. For example, they do not believe that faculty development programs should turn their efforts to supporting faculty in regard to outreach and service activities, community-based research, or faculty entrepreneurship. Ironically, because of declines in revenue at some institutions, faculty may feel pressure to bring in more external funding or to engage in activities that establish links with the broader public or external markets (Newman, Couturier, & Scurry, 2004). Faculty might feel ill-equipped to compete in this more entrepreneurial environment. While at most institutions faculty developers already have responsibilities that exceed their resources of time and energy, these findings should alert institutional leaders to consider how faculty members will be supported as they are encouraged to take on such new responsibilities and roles.

Conclusion

As faculty developers look to the future, they have recognized and have identified many of the issues and priorities that will require attention if faculty members, students, and institutions are to be well supported in meeting an array of responsibilities. How these issues will be addressed, given the many issues already requiring the attention of developers, is an important institutional challenge, which is considered more fully in the final chapter.

Chapter highlights

- In the coming years, the primary issues deserving attention through faculty development include changes in faculty roles and terms of employment, student learning, technology, and academic leadership and management.

- There are similarities among many of the challenges facing research/doctoral universities, comprehensive universities, and liberal arts colleges. Community colleges face different challenges that are closely linked to their unique mission.

- Faculty development is not meeting every challenge facing faculty. Institutional leaders will need to consider how faculty members will be supported as they take on new responsibilities and roles.

6

Future Directions for Faculty Development: Open-Ended Responses

T he future of faculty development won't just happen. Faculty, administrators, and faculty developers will create it through their action, or inaction, today. As we have argued throughout this book, challenges and opportunities lie ahead, and we will need to make farsighted decisions. By considering what *should* happen and what *might* happen, we can more thoughtfully decide on the most desirable future for faculty development and then work to achieve it.

At the end of our survey, we asked faculty developers to reflect on and respond to two open-ended questions: which directions they think the field of faculty development *should* move in the next decade and in which directions they think the field *will* move. Seventy-five percent of our respondents commented on these two questions, and their answers included a wide range of forecasts, alternative scenarios, and cautions. This chapter offers a snapshot of developers' views of future possibilities and probabilities for the field and highlights a number of the forces that will play a formative role in the future of faculty development. Through their own words, faculty developers form a picture that can help make sense out of the future.

This chapter presents a selection of developers' thoughts on each topic. Comments are given in full except where marked with ellipses; abbreviations have been expanded and occasional punctuation added for clarity. Except where respondents did not provide the information, each quote is followed by the respondent's title and institutional type.

In What Directions Should and Will the Field Move?

When developers were invited to write their own thoughts, they gave no absolute consensus regarding the directions in which the field of faculty development should move in the next decade. Though we categorized responses, our nearly 30 content codes still did not account for all the issues developers brought up as important areas that faculty development should be addressing through services and programs. Responses ranged from the expected—helping faculty integrate technology meaningfully into the classroom and deepening faculty involvement in and use of active and collaborative teaching and learning approaches—to the less predictable—building interdisciplinary connections and communities of practice among faculty or providing web-based faculty development. Overall, faculty developers identified five directions in which they thought the field should move. These new directions encompassed many of the key issues and priorities identified in Chapters 4 and 5, which highlighted developers' assessment of the importance of a range of issues listed in the survey. They include: helping faculty integrate technology meaningfully into the classroom; deepening faculty involvement in pedagogies of engagement; addressing the new, often expanding roles and responsibilities of faculty and helping faculty balance those roles; building interdisciplinary connections and communities of practice among faculty; and attending to issues of diversity at student, faculty, and institutional levels.

Comments regarding the direction in which the field of faculty development will move in the next decade contrasted strongly with the visions faculty developers had about where the field should move. Technology integration in higher education dominated responses about where the field will move. This issue was by no means welcomed without reservation as a primary focus for faculty development. Many developers expressed strong concerns about faculty development being relegated to technology assistance. While many saw the need to integrate technology in meaningful and appropriate ways into classroom and other learning situations, developers cautioned that not enough research was being done to determine what was meaningful and appropriate, and that their institutions were going forward applying technology in arbitrary and unreflective ways.

Assessment of student learning outcomes and of educational programs was the second most mentioned issue. Developers embraced classroom-based assessment and the scholarship-of-teaching movement, in which faculty engage in reflection and inquiry about their teaching practices. They expressed concern, however, about a shift from assessment for improving learning to assessment for accountability to satisfy the requirements of accreditation reviews or state mandates. Often technology and assessment were mentioned together, and juxtaposed negatively against respondents' visions for addressing the issues of integration and balance in faculty members' lives, championing active and collaborative learning, and engaging in the scholarship of teaching and faculty development.

The differences between what directions faculty development should move in and what directions faculty developers believe the field will move illustrate some of the tensions reflected overall in the survey. Faculty development programs, committees, and centers are not always able to engage in development efforts in the areas they see as most important and do not always see themselves as able to do so in the future. The open-ended comments provide evidence that there need to be more connections between where faculty developers envision the field moving and where they see it moving or being pushed by outside forces. Developers clearly desire more harmonious linkages.

The open-ended responses support the differences among institutions regarding priorities for faculty development. Respondents from all institutional types pointed to active, student-centered learning and technology integration as key areas needing attention in the future. Research university respondents (often directors of faculty development centers) were far more likely to see the future of faculty development needing to center on the promotion of organizational development and change (although they did not see it as a direction the field will take), and on becoming a more respected and credible voice in higher education, than respondents at other institutions, especially liberal arts and community colleges. Community college respondents want the field to address the needs of part-time faculty and to rethink the ways in which faculty development is structured and offered in their institutions more than they advocate for other issues. Respondents in these institutions were less focused on the need to build interdisciplinary communities of faculty, or to address the need to balance expanding faculty roles, than were liberal arts, comprehensive, and research institution respondents. Interestingly, community college respondents were the only ones to identify the need for web-based, online teaching and faculty development offerings as an important priority. Developers from other types of institutions were more hesitant about embracing what they saw as dehumanizing, technology-based approaches to teaching and learning and faculty development, and expressed more interest in reviving what they saw as personalized faculty development—face-to-face work with faculty, addressing the needs of the whole faculty member.

A Sample of Developers' Comments About Where the Field Should and Will Move

The selected comments presented here are organized around the topics developers most frequently mentioned in response to open-ended questions about directions in which the field of faculty development should move and will move.

Integrating technology into teaching and learning

I think we need to address new developments (e.g., technology) while not losing sight of our values and priorities (e.g., diversity).
—Assistant/Associate Director, Research/Doctoral Institution

Technology integration is one of the most pervasive forces influencing the field of faculty development and is inviting (forcing) higher education faculty to examine their past, present, and future pedagogies. This is one of the benefits of technology integration, despite its shortcomings and drawbacks. I also think integrating technology in effective ways is one way the field of faculty development should be and is moving; it will be the force, I believe, that will bring higher education faculty into developing their teaching further and will thereby provide greater credibility to the field of faculty development and teaching/learning centers.
—No title given, Research/Doctoral Institution

I believe that faculty development should reflect a "backlash" to the increased emphasis on technology. The "movement" should begin to or revive an emphasis on the personal relationships between teachers and students and the expansion of authentic learning communities.
—No title given, Research/Doctoral Institution

I fear in North America there will be greater emphasis on educational technology issues, online learning, distance education, etc. Outside the U.S. we'll see much more targeted development relating to market-driven educational priorities (this has already happened in Britain and Australia).
—Director, Research/Doctoral Institution

More technology integration—technology is a black hole in most campuses. It sucks in all available resources and time.
—Director, Comprehensive Institution

I think this hi-tech stuff is depersonalizing instruction. What I'm specifically referring to is distance-learning emphasis. It is a means to deal with students living a distance from a college/university, but not a means to an end. I think faculty development will move in this direction.

—Faculty Member, Community College

The emphasis on technology is likely to continue—I wish we could do better on knowing and integrating the most important aspects of technology.

—Director, Comprehensive Institution

Every job description includes a requirement for the faculty developer to understand the ever-increasing technology. It has become a basic requirement for the job. Some of the interpersonal skills may not be considered as basic.

—Director, Research/Doctoral Institution

Teaching for student-centered learning

I don't foresee much radical change. I think we need to keep on trying to help faculty engage their students more actively in learning. It's a difficult challenge for faculty and they need all the support and help they can get.

—Director, Research/Doctoral Institution

Student-centered learning should be key—I hope we bring about cultural change so that it becomes acceptable—even good—to discuss teaching with our colleagues as a problem-solving experience, rather than just for personnel decisions.

—Faculty Member, Comprehensive Institution

Put more energy into determining what student learning really means. Let's move beyond knowledge-based, skill-based, and cogni-

tive development objectives. . . . Meta-analysis (built upon well conceptualized empirical research) of online teaching methods. What facilitates student learning, what doesn't.

—Director, Comprehensive Institution

Although faculty developers may think "been there, done that," I do not think we are anywhere near getting faculty on board for "student-centered learning." I think [instructional, faculty, and organizational development] must carry the banner for student-centered everything!

—Assistant/Associate Director, Research/Doctoral Institution

In the past, many of our faculty could spend time developing basic instructional skills over time. However, the shift to learner-centered instruction, increased use of technologies, and the changing roles of instructors makes training in sound instructional basics absolutely essential. Most post-secondary institutions need to improve instructor readiness programs.

—Other, Community College

We will still need to address the basic principles of good instruction that is student focused but enhancing it through the use of new technologies and innovative technique.

—Director, Community College

[We need to] educate a greater percentage of faculty about the powerful new ideas about college teaching that have emerged in the last two decades.

—Director, Research/Doctoral Institution

Assessment of student learning outcomes

*Insofar as possible (and as local conditions permit) faculty develop-
ment should move more deliberately into the broader arenas of curriculum assessment, outcomes assessment, accreditation issues, and
the reform of graduate and undergraduate education. It is my
impression that most faculty development programs are excluded
from campus discussions of these kinds of issues, and our expertise is
going begging. If institutions come to recognize our expertise in these
areas, traditional faculty development activities will be more secure
and (perhaps) more easily accomplished.*
—Director, Research/Doctoral Institution

*I hope we can resist pressures to be part of the various evaluation sys-
tems politicians are so eager for: assessment, [post-tenure] review, etc.*
—Director, Research/Doctoral Institution

*Becoming increasingly cynical, probably will be limited to providing
lip-service (to all but the most dedicated faculty) to the requirements
set forth by the various accrediting bodies.*
—Faculty Member, Research/Doctoral Institution

*[Faculty development will go] in the directions of assessment and
technology—areas administrators find important or compelling for
"business" purposes rather than educational purposes.*
—Program Coordinator, Research/Doctoral Institution

*I worry that pressing student outcomes will drive faculty develop-
ment efforts.*
—Director, Comprehensive Institution

Integrating faculty roles

Balance and integration of faculty roles are huge issues. I think faculty development needs to focus on building faculty collegiality/community in teaching and research across departmental boundaries, helping figure out how to lead an integrated, balanced life; improving rewards and structures such as tenure and post-tenure review.
—Director, Research/Doctoral Institution

I think we should move toward providing more "holistic" support of the faculty member. It appears our primary focus has been on teaching performance. This can be expanded to include research, extension, and personal well-being.
—Senior Administrator, Research/Doctoral Institution

I think we need to move away from the term "faculty" development and move toward a more inclusive concept of "professional" development that better reflects the diversity of roles (i.e., entrepreneur, consultant, etc.) of twenty-first-century college and university faculty.
—Senior Administrator, Other American Institution

This is the unknown. While campuses "talk the talk" they don't seem to be "walking the walk." There is much lamenting of the state of higher education but we seem locked into a black box mentally where we can't see a way out. To create the environment that's needed to produce a flourishing campus environment will need creative solutions that don't seem to be forthcoming. We know what's needed for vibrant campuses but we don't know how to pay for it and there's the rub. Unless the reward and tenure system changes there will be no future direction, we'll just keep struggling the way we are. Unless we define the role of professor differently (perhaps separate it from researcher), we will always struggle with too much to do with too little time and too little preparation.
—Director, Research/Doctoral Institution

[I hope to see] a more integrative view of faculty work and life—integrating stages of professional development, integrating skills with philosophy and attitudes, integrating scholarship with teaching.
—No title given, Research/Doctoral Institution

Greater integration of the many types of faculty development—all of these activities (advising, technology, teaching, etc.) that make up a faculty role—need to be supported.
—Director, Research/Doctoral Institution

New and part-time faculty members

Continue to support the future professoriate through graduate student teaching development; get more involved in fostering collaborative peer review and faculty mentoring; foster the use of teaching portfolios for formative evaluations of teaching; get involved in the evaluation of student learning outcomes in distributed learning efforts. (All these can be subsumed under the Scholarship of Faculty Development.)
—No title given, Research/Doctoral Institution

With high numbers of retirements, faculty development should focus on the new generation of faculty. If these new faculty can be assisted to develop a culture of teaching and learning that is student centered, then there is great hope for the future.
—Program Coordinator, Research/Doctoral Institution

Capitalize on the ripple effect of Preparing Future Faculty support by identifying new faculty who have participated in PFF programs and enlisting their support and expertise.
—No title given, Research/Doctoral Institution

. . . Community colleges—and some universities—face immense change and turnover as administrators and faculty retire. The next decade will stretch both the staff and resources for faculty development. Like others in post-secondary education, many faculty developers will leave their positions. Big question: are we adequately preparing the next generation?

—Director, Community College

Given the proportional role of adjuncts in teaching underprepared students—faculty development for these folks would benefit students and their own career development.

—Director, Comprehensive Institution

Unfortunately, the increasing use of part-time faculty will create enormous (and increasing) stress on institutional budget priorities. This is particularly true of the community colleges.

—No title given, Community College

Interdisciplinary connections and communities of practice

[I hope to see] collaborative work to break down barriers between groups and allow them to learn from each other and expand their creativity, understanding of others, and overall enjoyment at work.

—Assistant/Associate Director, Research/Doctoral Institution

A focus on building interdisciplinary teams and programs integrating technology and service-learning [equals] community.

—Director, Research/Doctoral Institution

On our campus a recent discussion on spirituality in the classroom resulted in record attendance—this speaks strongly to the need that

faculty are feeling (and, in many cases, students). There is a need to come together and explore our role at deeper levels. Of course this clashes with the current education-as-business attitude. Yet we need to find a way to be accountable, to provide an educated citizenry, to be fiscally responsible, but not lose the essence of who we are and what we are here for. We need to more clearly define the balance in faculty life—there is no time yet there must be time or else we may create an assembly line approach to education.

—Director, Research/Doctoral Institution

Connect faculty, students, and alumni for mutual benefit in both teaching and learning. When we survey our students, they want advice and mentoring in regard to courses, learning, future goals, civic endeavors, etc. I think we need to build coalitions and collaborations between public schools, universities, faculty and students, and other interested persons to enrich teaching, learning, service, and research.

—No title given, Research/Doctoral Institution

I think faculty development programs need to work to more actively link themselves with programs and initiatives on their campuses. It seems to me those programs which are most successful are those where they are working in partnership in applied ways with other areas on the campus. Examples include situations where faculty development programs link with learning communities and service-learning programs, general education revisions, etc. Ultimately, it needs to help define new structures and ways of operating organizationally.

—No title given, Other American Institution

. . . In our institution, at least, I'd like to see more acknowledgment of the faculty as learners, too. There is an attitude of denial about any need for development on the part of many, including key administrators . . .

—Director, Research/Doctoral Institution

Diversity

[We need to] address disparities in who teaches and who is taught (racially). Addressing disparities in who teaches and who is taught (diversity) . . .

—Faculty Member, No institution listed

[Work] toward helping faculty prepare students for life and work in a culturally diverse environment.

—Faculty Member, No institution listed

Faculty developers should be more collaborative within the university, should infuse multiculturalism into their work, and should exemplify scholarly, research-based practice.

—Director, No institution listed

[We should] help faculty cope with demands, embrace changes resulting from infusion of technology, [and] "humanize" higher education to be more responsive to the needs of ever more diverse student learners (both traditional and nontraditionally aged).

—Director, Research/Doctoral Institution

. . . [We should] get more faculty involved in meeting the needs of diverse (underprepared, disengaged?) learners—through active learning strategies, classroom assessment, and mentoring . . .

—No title given, Research/Doctoral Institution

[We should] teach strategies for multiple learning styles and levels. Teach for students who respond to technology and media intensive learning.

—Other, Liberal Arts

The Future of the Field

For approximately 30 years, the Professional and Organizational Network in Higher Education (POD Network) has advocated for the ongoing enhancement of teaching and learning through faculty development. In 2003 the POD Network crafted a vision statement for the 21st century that charges the organization to "expand guidelines for educational development, build strong alliances with sister organizations, and encourage developer exchanges and research projects to improve teaching and learning" (Core Committee, April 2003). In the open-ended comments of our study, developers offered a number of insights on what *should* and what *will* be the vision for the future of the field of faculty development. Their comments elaborate and expand on the vision of the POD Network.

Developers' visions about the future of the field coalesced around three key areas. Many called for more emphasis on organizational development and change. They believe that developers should take a stronger leadership role within higher education institutions, becoming involved in governance structures, aligning their centers with institutional priorities, engaging in discussions of reward structures, and working with academic leaders. There was also a sense among developers that faculty development should work to gain more respect and credibility as a field or discipline of study. Credibility and respect were linked to the field's ability to articulate a body of scholarly knowledge, standards, and core competencies that defines it, and to build on the research base already laid for the scholarship of teaching.

There was some commentary on the merits of restructuring faculty development—by making it more central and valued, by diversifying development offerings and efforts, or by integrating faculty development into departments or interdisciplinary groups. Some developers expressed the view that faculty development should be spread throughout institutions and that departments and individuals could take up faculty development themselves. Others argued that the field should proactively network with external organizations—accreditation bodies and other higher education associations, such as the Carnegie Foundation for the Advancement of Teaching and Learning and the American Association for Higher Education.

Developers also believe that the field of faculty development and its place in higher education institutions will gain credibility and respect in the coming years, although there is also a sense that funding issues will be important. Many faculty expressed the belief that centers and programs within institutions would need to fund their own efforts from external sources, while others believed that internal funding would come with the increased stature of faculty development within colleges and universities.

Also evident in the open-ended responses were two competing positions regarding who owns faculty development. One position (expressed most often by liberal arts and comprehensive university respondents) was that faculty should own their own development. A number of respondents at liberal arts colleges expressed a vision of faculty development planned and decided by the faculty themselves—that faculty development without faculty input was not faculty development. Similarly, many respondents at comprehensive institutions saw their role as serving faculty rather than administrative interests and needs.

The other position was that institutional administrations own faculty development, for better or worse. Some respondents argued that faculty development should be more aligned with and responsive to the critical needs of the institution, needs often defined by the campus administration. Many noted that faculty development must work to be a more legitimate, central, and respected part of the institution. But the drawback to such alignments also emerged, especially in concerns about being pushed into an overemphasis on technology without careful consideration of issues such as course content and student and faculty readiness. Responses to earlier survey questions regarding who establishes the priorities for faculty development support this sense that the faculty development agenda is set, in part, by the priorities perceived by senior-level administrators. Some respondents were somewhat negative or resigned about this situation. Others were more positive in their view that the strongest faculty development programs were those that responded to the needs of both faculty and institutional leaders in setting agendas for development.

Developers also grappled with the issue of who they think belongs in faculty development. Comments about who faculty developers should be and how they should (or should not) be trained or prepared for their profession pointed to a tension between a perceived need to professionalize the field and a concern that doing so will diminish it.

Numerous developers saw the need for faculty development to be more discipline-like, with a defined body of scholarly knowledge, core competencies, skills, and practices. Some desired more formal pathways into the profession, such as specific graduate training and continuing professional education. Many also felt the need for the field to engage in more research about best practices that influence student learning, and to work programmatically from a research base on teaching and learning. In contrast, some developers were adamant that pushing for creation of a disciplinary field of faculty development would be, as one developer argued, "the kiss of death" to the enterprise, gutting it of its unique perspective in favor of "methods." Another argued that the field should retain its "big tent" approach, with multiple paths into the profession.

In conclusion, respondents expressed a range of visions for the future of faculty development—the issues they saw as important to address were by no means focused exclusively on issues of teaching and learning, although those issues remained primary concerns. They saw the need to address other issues faculty face as they confront expanding roles, competing responsibilities, and the demand for new skills. Faculty developers, especially directors of centers at larger institutions, called for faculty development to take a more prominent role in institutional development and strategic change, and to raise the credibility, importance, and centrality of faculty development in their institutions among both administrators and faculty.

The most striking theme to emerge from the open-ended responses was the desire for more connection between where participants wished to see faculty development move and where they saw it moving, with or without their control. Respondents were deeply concerned about what they saw as an over-reliance on technology as the teaching and learning "fix" that everyone must use, and their role as technology consultants to faculty subsuming all other roles and issues they see as important to address. They also worried about increasing pressure on the field to be part of the assessment movement and various evaluation processes such as accreditation reviews and post-tenure review.

Perhaps most interesting was developers' sense that they need to find better ways to manage or direct these shifts in focus in the future. They are concerned about how they will address both the perceived needs of senior administrators and the expressed needs of faculty. And many also want a voice in creating their own framework for understanding the role of faculty development in the future—what it is, why it is important, who the key players will be, what future developments to expect, and how to chart a course for that future.

A Sample of Developers' Comments About the Future of the Field

We offer a selection of comments from developers that capture their hopes, concerns, and ideas about the future of faculty development as a field.

Organizational development

More collaborations, work with administrators as partners, being leaders, souls of the institutions (call people on some questionable practices and values). We need to be more driven by the big picture and questions and fundamental values.
—Program Coordinator, Research/Doctoral Institution

After twenty-some years in the POD Network, I have finally come to agree with my few POD colleagues who have argued for years that we have neglected the "O" in POD—i.e., we need to focus much more on helping ensure the "health" of colleges and universities as functional organizations.
—No title given, No institution listed

Toward greater emphasis on interpersonal dynamics, sensitivity, avoiding lawsuits, and maintaining morale in departments. Helping chairs support their faculty and maintain high standards.
—No title given, Comprehensive Institution

. . . Supporting and training management to deal with the stresses of the changing higher education environment—a) there aren't enough of us, b) the changes are too big, c) with change comes opportunity to influence direction for years to come . . .
—Director, Comprehensive Institution

Play a more prominent role in the institution's strategic planning. Play a bigger role in developing leadership abilities in faculty. Participate in defining an institution's post-tenure review policy and practice.
—Faculty Member, Comprehensive Institution

We need to learn more about the variables that influence an organization's culture and how we can exert some influence on those variables.
—Director, Other American Institution

One of the difficult issues those of us face in faculty development . . . is the lack of concern by the administration, and many faculty members who are not initiated now feel the need for this learning and growing experience.
—Director, Liberal Arts

Greater emphasis on working with chairs and deans to create environments that support good teaching and scholarship. Faculty live in their departments and schools. While changes can be implemented university-wide, the quickest and most profound changes will occur through departments and schools. From my experience at several universities, there are usually a few departments which are dysfunctional, resulting in personal pain and little development. Careful selections of chairs and deans is important, but fostering their own growth as leaders is critical.
—Director, Research/Doctoral Institution

Recognition and credibility for the field

The field will stay largely marginalized until we contribute more research and scholarly work valued by our peers.
—Director, Research/Doctoral Institution

Faculty development needs to finesse the research we have on teaching and learning into practice. I think I can help and be helped by others in similar [Research 1] institutions who write up intelligent and vocabulary-sensitive pieces about what they are doing and can

do with their faculty and institutions. There is not much that is so heavily data-rich and dense that I can have my faculty (all liberal arts) read first hand.
—Director, Research/Doctoral Institution

At least in my college, faculty development is seen as "fluff"—a nice entity that is politically correct to have but expendable. It should be a foundation for faculty—a strong voice and educational anchor.
—Faculty Member, Comprehensive Institution

As someone attempting to do faculty development at a medical teaching center, I find that "faculty development" is often the first thing cut when budgets are tight. Health care financing is in crisis and this greatly affects the ability to train teachers within health and medical professions.
—Director, Research/Doctoral Institution

1) Leadership institutions will continue to move forward, and others will slowly get on board just to keep up. 2) The struggle to be number one in research will likely continue to eclipse the importance of teaching, sadly. 3) Those of us in faculty development will continue to network and learn from each other, thus legitimizing our work more and more.
—Director, Research/Doctoral Institution

More and more faculty are going to be seeking services and programs regarding their development (in the areas of teaching, research, and service) as the "stigma" associated with faculty development as remedial wanes. For those centers that listen to what services and programs faculty want, new initiatives will be created and the faculty centers will notice a substantial improvement in their ability to influence the campus culture.
—Other, Research/Doctoral Institution

. . . Where will faculty development move? I'm not sure what I'd pre-dict. I hope better qualified people will move into faculty develop-ment positions. I hope some graduate programs can have an empha-sis in this area—maybe it needs to have the word "management" in it to have a respectable draw?

—Senior Administrator, Comprehensive Institution

Over the years I have had a sort of love-hate relationship with facul-ty development—why are the units so marginalized? Underfunded? Understaffed? Why aren't the new initiatives/interests "assigned" to these units? Why haven't we been able to show more results? A lot of the problem, I think, is that the field . . . always goes in the same direction. I only go to [the POD Network's annual conference] every 2–3 years now and since I started going in the early 1980s the pro-gram is exactly the same. It seems as though there is nothing new under the sun for faculty development—that the field has not matured and moved forward to influence the teaching and learning agenda in higher education. . . . I'm still concerned that faculty developers have no professional credentials—you can't get a Ph.D. in faculty development anywhere, can you? We need to know a lot more about who we are. I'm also concerned about burnout—some of us have/did. I'm only minimally back after six years of not leading a cen-ter. What do we know about the faculty developer's career trajectory?

—Faculty Member, Liberal Arts

Professionalization of the field

I think that we should think about preparation and development of people in our field, and begin to create degree programs designed to prepare professionals to do faculty development and to contribute to the theoretical foundations of the field through research. I have heard people discuss the "theory of writing centers" but never the "theory of

faculty development centers." We should begin to grow in that direction.
—Director, Research/Doctoral Institution

The "field" should be more defined, "professionalized." The scholarship of faculty development needs to be further developed to support this (e.g., through the International Journal for Academic Development).
—Assistant/Associate Director, Comprehensive Institution

Faculty development will become more professional and credible. It has to in order to survive and make a difference.
—Program Coordinator, Research/Doctoral Institution

I think the field of faculty development will move in the direction of increasing professionalization, with an emphasis on technique and technology. As I look at job descriptions and the directions of centers of teaching, there is an increasing emphasis on methodological and technological support for teaching. The faculty development professional of the future will be interested in methods more than ideas with a heavy emphasis on technology. . . . If faculty development does not attend to the whole person of the faculty member and [his or her] development, then we will move into a state analogous to the early days of writing clinics, in which faculty development becomes a fix-it shop to improve faculty rather than a locus for self-discovery, high aspirations, and enriching the lives of faculty and through them the students we teach.
—Director, Liberal Arts

Scholarship of teaching, learning, and faculty development

We should build a scholarship base for our faculty development work. We should encourage faculty in their pedagogical content knowledge and scholarship of teaching . . .
—Director, Research/Doctoral Institution

Using the scholarship of teaching to encourage faculty to honestly consider their approach to facilitating learning—believing there likely is a better approach . . .
—Faculty Member, Research/Doctoral Institution

Research-based teaching in two areas: 1) basing practice on what research tells us about the nature of learning and behavior, and 2) bringing students into the process of research and inquiry.
—No title given, Research/Doctoral Institution

Toward the affirmation of "a scholarship of teaching." It will take tireless efforts to transform the culture of the academy from the current priority of research to one that actually valorizes pedagogy. Even in colleges of education, teaching is hardly the high priority.
—Faculty Member, Comprehensive Institution

I think that the whole scholarship of teaching and learning movement is incredibly valuable in that it can change our campus cultures in very positive ways to support and elevate teaching and learning and create more reflective practice. The issue of integrating good pedagogy with instructional technology is also a crucial one. Finally, focusing on student learning outcomes rather than on teaching "innovation."
—Director, Other American Institution

Changing faculty development structures

I think faculty development programs need to work to more actively link themselves with programs and initiatives on their campuses. It seems to me those programs which are most successful are those where they are working in partnership in applied ways with other areas on the campus. Examples include situations where faculty development programs link with learning communities and service-learning programs, general education revisions, etc. Ultimately it needs to help define new structures and ways of operating organizationally.
—No title given, Other American Institution

Finding entry points into the belief systems of faculty members— learning how to create opportunities to bring together those who think there is nothing to learn about teaching with those who reflect frequently, and engaging all in real dialogue about teaching.
—Director, Canadian Institution

Faculty development must be flexible enough to move in the direction indicated by faculty needs. Further communication is needed between faculty development departments and faculty.
—Faculty Member, Canadian Institution

Continuing to keep faculty involved in the administration of faculty development is key. Faculty know what they need and what priorities will aid them. They need to continue to have ownership of the faculty development process. With teaching and learning centers becoming more prominent, we must work to find the balance between these two important centers in higher education.
—No title given, Liberal Arts

We're in what Kuhn called pre-paradigmatic empiricism—things will move in all sorts of directions depending on local context and personalities. I think it will shake out into more functional, task-specific support rather than the big centralized generalized faculty development centers—and it will be more faculty-run!
                                        —Director, Comprehensive Institution

I think we will move from micromanaging to macro or proactive planning—from smaller to larger.
                    —Instructional Development Consultant, Comprehensive Institution

We also need to start making connections among the various initiatives (e.g., scholarship of teaching, diversity, assessment). I think the field and the POD Network need to find ways to be at the table for discussions at both the national and, perhaps more challenging, at the institutional level.
                        —Assistant/Associate Director, Research/Doctoral Institution

Funding issues

Because of the cost of faculty development programs, we will need to generate good data that show the cost effectiveness of the programs.
                                    —Senior Administrator, No institution listed

I'm afraid in this climate, [faculty development] will be cut back, so we do less rather than more. Faculty will use technology more, and that will affect our work.
                                —Director, Research/Doctoral Institution

Less money, more careful spending, new ways to raise funds. More open and honest dialogue with all constituencies to find out what they want. We are going to have to serve our faculty in ways that address their needs. More service to underrepresented groups—but what they perceive is their need. We will need to embrace good change and we will need to innovate and create new programs which connect us all. Our state is really looking at what kind of citizens our universities are training.

—Other, Research/Doctoral Institution

Faculty have little time to further investigate courses offered by faculty development or apply for grants which require a convoluted and complex application system. In an institution like ours, the people who have the time to follow rigorous application protocols are the support staff.

—Faculty Member, Canadian Institution

. . . We are caught in the business model of education. We need to think more about the common good as opposed to individual wealth and well being.

—Instructional Development Consultant, Community College

Chapter highlights

- When asked to share their thoughts about the future of faculty development, developers indicated that the field should move in the direction of technology integration, pedagogies of engagement, faculty roles, interdisciplinary communities, and diversity.

- Essential questions about the role of technology integration in teaching and learning and the uses of assessment for improvement and reporting to external audiences will be paramount for the field to address.

- Enhancing the future of the field of faculty development will require more emphasis on organizational development and change, professionalization of the field, and new thinking about ideal structures for faculty development.

7

Faculty Development in the Age of the Network

U niversities and colleges live in a world of changing expectations, multiple demands, and issues of access, new knowledge and skills, globalization, competition, accountability, multiculturalism, and the influence of technology (Newman, Couturier, & Scurry, 2004). In this challenging environment, faculty development should be one of colleges' and universities' most significant priorities. Faculty are being asked to strengthen their teaching and research, to transform their instruction to fit a learning-centered rather than teaching-centered paradigm, and to work with an increasingly diverse student body. They must become more agile in learning new technologies and in designing and delivering curricula, even as they are being asked to create more sophisticated measures of student success. Support for faculty members as they take on new roles is an issue of critical importance to all institutions of higher education. Both institutional leaders and professionals in the field of faculty development must think carefully about what purposes faculty development should serve and what forms it should take as the 21st century unfolds.

This concluding chapter begins by recapping the key findings from the research reported in this book. It reflects on changes in faculty development across four ages—the Age of the Scholar, the Age of the Teacher, the Age of the Developer, and the Age of the Learner. It offers a benchmark of faculty development as we enter the latest age—the Age of the Network—an age in which faculty, academic leaders, and faculty developers will need to connect, communicate, and collaborate to meet the challenge of how to do more with less while simultaneously maintaining excellence. We highlight developers' perspectives on important future directions and raise questions suggested by our investigation of the challenges and opportunities for faculty development in the coming years. These questions are worthy of consideration by faculty developers and by other academic leaders.

Mark Twain is said to have remarked that the art of prophecy is difficult, especially with respect to the future. We do not offer a tidy model or a clear blueprint for the future of faculty development. Institutions function in a dynamic, changing environment and vary considerably in their primary missions, their faculty demographics, the characteristics of their students, the teaching and learning modes they employ, and the communities they serve. Nevertheless, we believe that the field of faculty development is poised to take a significant step forward.

Thus, we offer a working agenda to help guide faculty development in the new century. Our field stands on a distinguished history of dedication to helping faculty members improve their work as scholars, teachers, and learners. We envision that faculty development will offer faculty members higher levels of knowledge and skill as they grapple with new and different roles. The opportunity for faculty development to contribute to the broader success of institutions has never been greater, and we envision that faculty development efforts will become associated even more clearly than at the present with *institutional* commitment to excellence and quality. Admittedly, the future offers a multitude of challenges, but it also offers more opportunities for faculty development than ever before. In this last chapter, we actively look to those opportunities, and call upon faculty and other academic leaders to further imagine with us the future of faculty development.

The First Four Ages

In Chapter 1 we traced the evolution of faculty development through the first four ages. In the Age of the Scholar, the term *faculty development* was synonymous with activities to improve scholarly competence. There were few formal faculty development programs and even fewer studies of faculty development efforts. In the Age of the Teacher, faculty development expanded to include faculty, instructional, and organizational development. Faculty continued to value scholarly support but also grew more interested in teaching development activities. In the United States, faculty development professionalized as a field through the creation of two associations: the Professional and Organizational Development Network in Higher Education (POD Network) and the National Council for Staff, Program, and Organizational Development (NCSPOD).

The Age of the Developer saw an increase in faculty participation in teaching and curricular development projects. The field broadened to include activities supportive of faculty across career stages, sponsored by foundations and institutional funds, and encouraging of collaborative and individual development. Faculty development became more than an American concern with the development of the Society for Teaching and Learning in Higher Education (STLHE) in Canada.

During the Age of the Learner, the number of teaching and learning centers continued to increase across all types of institutions, and their goals, scope of activities, and impact also expanded. Other associations, private foundations, and professional societies began to sponsor their own faculty development initiatives. And perhaps most revealing, countries around the globe launched faculty development consortiums, institutes, and societies.

At the cusp of the Age of the Network, we can mark a number of dramatic changes in the field since its beginnings. Over the decades, faculty development has proven its capacity to anticipate and respond to changes in higher education. It has opened opportunities for teaching as well as scholarly development. It has recognized changes in students—their increasing diversity, their different learning needs, and their new demands as consumers of education. It has evolved from a focus on individual to collective development and from singular to multidimensional purposes. From little coordination, there has been tremendous growth in centralized units across all types of institutions, offering more opportunities for collegial dialogues, integrated services, and responsiveness to teaching excellence. Faculty development has become a professional field; its community of developers has expanded from a small band of brothers and sisters to more than 1,400 members. And those members have expanded their expertise in individual, course, and program development, student-centered learning, multicultural education, assessment, and instructional technology. Professional societies, associations, and foundations increasingly support and engage in faculty development initiatives. Perhaps most exciting, faculty development has become a global concern. In country after country, new centers are opening and new approaches to teaching, learning, and faculty development are evolving. This development offers the promise of greater levels of collaboration, knowledge and skill exchange, and mutual understanding among nations as we enter the Age of the Network.

Key Priorities in the Age of the Network

The Age of the Network is inextricably linked to the Ages of the Scholar, Teacher, Developer, and Learner in powerful ways. Specifically, a number of the key issues, challenges, and new directions identified by faculty developers in this study are mirrored in earlier challenges and opportunities for change. The interactive effects among the five ages are profound and ongoing. Yet in the Age of the Network the challenges and opportunities appear more intensified and complex, and they hold significant implications for the future of higher education. It is impossible for faculty development to address them alone; solutions will require active linkages among stakeholders that result in expanded networks operating at many levels.

A myriad of issues that faculty developers indicated were important to address through faculty development and a number of new challenges and pressures on institutions that affect faculty work emerge from Chapters 4, 5, and 6. This constellation of issues seemed to coalesce around three primary forces of change:

- The changing professoriate
- The changing student body
- The changing nature of teaching, learning, and scholarship

Faculty developers in our study indicate that the Age of the Network will be an especially demanding time for the professoriate. They describe faculty members as being in the midst of transformational changes to their traditional roles and tasks. Furthermore, many faculty members are no longer in traditional full-time, tenure-stream positions. Respondents in our study see faculty development as a central strategy for assisting faculty in balancing multiple responsibilities and taking on new and different roles. In looking across academic ranks and career stages, developers are calling for enhanced investment in resources to socialize and support a new, more diverse faculty, including more nontenure-track, part-time, and adjunct faculty. They suggest that leadership training should be provided for faculty members who move into administrative roles. Specifically, they are interested in ways that faculty development might operate at an organizational level in supporting department chairs and other academic leaders to ensure that they are prepared to respond to expectations and changes within the faculty ranks.

Early evidence of the impact of the Age of the Network can also be found in developers' attention to a changing student body. Faculty developers are well aware that students enrolling at their campuses are more diverse than in the past (in race, ethnicity, class, age, sexual orientation, preparation, and prior academic performance) and require a variety of services. Developers report that they are committed to doing more to assist faculty members in appreciating the diversity represented by their students and in responding with a range of effective strategies for teaching and facilitating student learning. While developers believe faculty development should help faculty members understand and work more effectively with all students, they are especially concerned about underprepared students, who may need work in college-level reading, writing, and computational skills. They report that preparing such students for success is a key challenge, but they also see the academic success of such students as tied to the success of their institutions.

Changes in the traditional environment for teaching, learning, and scholarship are clearly influencing developers' perspectives on pressing challenges to address in the Age of the Network. The old paradigm of teaching as the transmission of information through a low-tech lecture system is under siege, and it is hard to imagine that it will endure without significant change. It is gratifying to report that developers are actively working with faculty not only to improve traditional teaching methods such as the lecture and discussion, but also to further develop and support alternative instructional methods and tools. Faculty developers have taken the lead in promoting and enhancing student-centered learning, active and problem-based learning, the wide use of instructional technology, course-based assessment of student learning outcomes, the scholarship of teaching, and writing across the curriculum. They believe it is important that their programs continue to focus on these issues.

As we enter the Age of the Network, faculty developers have identified three areas that are driving change and shaping the future of faculty development. The impact of the changing professoriate is a major factor. How to develop and sustain the vitality of all of our faculty—newcomers, mid-career, senior, and part-timers—is a critical question that will need to be further explored and addressed through faculty development. A second factor is the increasingly diverse student body. It will be more important to invest in faculty development as a means of ensuring that we cultivate teachers, students, and campus environments that value diverse ideas, beliefs, and worldviews, promote community, and cultivate more inclusive student learning environments. According to developers, the third shaping influence is the impact of a changing paradigm for teaching, learning, and scholarly pursuits. The cumulative impact of these forces is transforming the field. Faculty development will require a larger investment of imagination and resources in order to strategically plan for and address new developments (e.g., teaching for student-centered learning, retention, learning technologies, assessment, increasing research demands) while not losing sight of core values and priorities.

An Emerging Agenda

The findings from this study raise critical questions for both faculty developers and the field of faculty development. The POD Network has already been engaged in extensive discussion over the past several years about the future of the profession and what leadership and support the organization should undertake to enhance the work of faculty developers and their institutions (Sell, 2002). We hope our work will contribute to the POD Network's continuing attention to the future of the field. Other venues for discussion might be the Special Interest Group on Faculty Development and Evaluation, which meets at the annual meeting of the American Educational Research Association. Groups that bring together administrative leaders, such as the Association of American Colleges and Universities and the American Council on Education, might also take up these questions.

In the future, one model or framework for faculty development will not be appropriate for all institutions. Instead, institutional leaders and faculty developers at each university or college must consider specific institutional and faculty needs within their own context and make choices appropriate for specific situations. However, we offer a working agenda that we believe can usefully guide faculty developers and the field of faculty development in higher education institutions in North America and beyond. This agenda builds on the distinguished history that has contributed to the dedicated faculty development work in place at many institutions today. It incorporates the many valuable insights shared with us by the faculty, administrators, and other members of the POD Network who responded to our survey.

This agenda also highlights issues that we hope will be in the forefront as provosts, deans, and other senior institutional administrative leaders, faculty governance leaders, and faculty development professionals engage in planning for the future.

Our goal is to move seamlessly from agenda items for faculty developers to agenda items for the field of faculty development. We found seven agenda items that are interrelated rather than discrete. Each item is followed by a short discussion and a set of questions. We envision that the questions can be especially useful to two audiences. Faculty development professionals may use them to guide periodic review of their work and planning for the future, while senior institutional leaders—provosts and their staff and faculty governing bodies—will find them useful as a springboard for thoughtful analysis and discussion of institutional attention to faculty development as a strategic lever for enhancing institutional excellence.

Promote professional preparation and development

Over the last 30 years, opportunities for professional development for faculty developers have been growing, and there are now annual conferences, intensive workshops, and summer institutes that feature best practices in the field. Opportunities like these will become even more critical, particularly given the changes in faculty roles, instructional technologies, and other emerging models for learning, teaching, and scholarly pursuits. Our study shows that a surprisingly large cohort of developers, including directors and administrators, are new to the field. This finding raises questions about the professional preparation and continuing development of practitioners in the field. We believe that this issue merits sustained attention so that faculty developers can better support faculty and institutions in their efforts to grow and change.

Questions for Consideration

- How can faculty developers best prepare to support faculty members in times of considerable change and expanding expectations?

- What is the appropriate role for faculty development professionals and for faculty development as a professional field in the current environment?

- How can individuals be best prepared to begin careers in faculty development?

- Should the field identify core competencies for faculty developers? Should it move in the direction of increased professionalization with special institutes, graduate degree programs, continuing education, etc.?

- What are the possible career paths for faculty development professionals? How can they be most effectively supported in their career growth?

- What are the responsibilities of the POD Network, NCSPOD, STLHE, and other regional, national, and international faculty development organizations for providing training for new developers, ongoing networks and professional development for experienced developers, and enhanced services for all their members?

Inform practice with scholarship

We believe that faculty development is most effective when enlightened by the scholarship concerning faculty careers, professional development, and work experiences, as well as the scholarship of organizational development and change. For decades, faculty developers have contributed to and based their practices on the research literature concerning faculty work and careers. This literature has provided a scholarly and theoretical basis to guide developers as they make choices about where interventions are most useful, how to support faculty professional growth, and what strategies are likely to be most effective.

Our study reveals that developers are most influenced by literature and research in college teaching and learning and faculty development, and less influenced by broader research in higher education, organizational development, adult development, human resources, and personal development. And yet literature and scholarship on organizational change and transformation in higher education and the implications for faculty work and development can expand developers' knowledge base on how best to prepare aspiring faculty members, how new faculty adjust to diverse and changing work environments, how established faculty learn new roles and adapt to new challenges, the specific needs of faculty in varying types of work appointments, and the implications of an array of organizational changes for faculty careers. Our findings also suggest that developers would welcome more opportunities for scholarly reflection on practice. In sum, building our scholarly acumen and building a defined body of scholarly knowledge for our field are unfinished agendas.

Questions for Consideration

- How can faculty developers stay current with an expanding research base on academic work, faculty careers, adult learning, organizational change, and teaching, learning, and faculty development?

- How can faculty developers best integrate ongoing research into practice?

- How can faculty developers continue to acquire and maintain skills and resources in order to research, write, and disseminate findings to more broadly inform practice?

- How can institutions offer opportunities for developers (e.g., exchanges, conferences, scholarly leaves) so that they can share state-of-the-art knowledge and practices on a broad array of issues in higher education with faculty and academic leaders?

- How can faculty development professional organizations encourage avenues for research and innovative practice in ways that will help to strengthen the profession?

- How can faculty development professional organizations provide more direct support to developers in institutions (e.g., print and web-based resources)?

Broaden the scope of faculty development

As a group, American colleges and universities have historically had three missions—teaching, research, and service. The particular emphasis and configuration of missions at any particular college or university depend on institutional type, history, and context, and an institution's faculty development planning should be matched to the missions the institution seeks to fulfill. Thus, in institutions that are expanding or reframing their missions, adjustments may be necessary to ensure that faculty members have the abilities and support to fulfill the expectations they face. Expectations should be coupled with support. Linking faculty development to institutional missions thus becomes a key element in an institution's strategic plan.

Our study indicates that many faculty development programs focus primarily on enhancing teaching and learning. This is important because college teaching (and learning) has become increasingly more difficult and complex, requiring new skills from faculty members and faculty developers. But for institutions to succeed in fulfilling their multiple missions, faculty members must be supported in all the roles they are asked to fulfill. Sometimes they will need to learn new skills or expand into new areas—new approaches to teaching, new ways to engage with communities, and new strategies or collaborations to pursue their research. It is clear from our findings that faculty developers appreciate the wide range of challenges facing faculty in terms of expanding roles. But who will support faculty as they add roles such as mentoring, advising, grant-getting, technology training, accreditation, outreach activities, and entrepreneurship to the traditional "three legs of the stool"?

Faculty development professionals have expert knowledge to offer and should be key participants in institutional decision-making about how best to support faculty work. At many institutions, faculty development centers will continue to be the most effective way to focus institutional resources and attention to faculty members' professional needs. But developers alone cannot address all the challenges and pressures affecting faculty members. Faculty development that is strategically planned and shared across the institution is likely to be most effective in the current context. Colleges and universities should consider how challenges concerning faculty work can best be addressed through faculty development efforts or through coordination with other units on campus.

Well-conceptualized faculty development plans recognize that institutional responses to changing expectations imply new roles and responsibilities for faculty members. When faculty development helps faculty members strengthen their abilities and skills, those efforts are simultaneously enhancing the excellence of the institution.

Questions for Consideration

- Given your institutional missions and the characteristics and needs of your faculty, what are the purposes of faculty development at your institution?

- To what extent is your institution's faculty development program aligned with the missions of the institution (e.g., teaching, research, service/outreach)?

- What are the gaps in how the institution is supporting faculty work across the institution's missions?

- How can your faculty development program work in partnership with other units (e.g., student affairs, research affairs, graduate school, academic planning and assessment) to further mutual agendas for enhancing student and faculty cultures?

- How can your faculty development program work with department chairs, deans, and other academic leaders to further mutual agendas (e.g., curriculum change and development, program assessment, the integration of instructional technology)?

Link individual and institutional needs

Our view is that the role and function of faculty development is to foster the growth and development of individual faculty members and of institutions. We cannot really support faculty in their work without considering department, college, or campus policies and practices. Similarly, we cannot design successful faculty development plans without considering the professional development of individual faculty members. Our study provides evidence that, in shaping and guiding their programs, faculty developers are highly influenced by the needs of individual faculty members and considerably less influenced by departmental and college needs, or by the critical needs and strategic goals defined by their institutions. While there will always be a creative and dynamic tension between individual and institutional needs, faculty developers will be well served by attending not only to the interests of the individual faculty member or special interest groups (e.g., newly hired tenure-track faculty) but also to larger institutional concerns. Such concerns depend upon institutional type and culture but might include retention, curriculum assessment, learning outcomes assessment, accreditation issues, faculty review processes, and the reform of graduate and undergraduate education.

A strategic approach would involve institutional leaders working with faculty members and faculty developers to examine the most important challenges and new pressures confronting each specific institution, given its history, students, and mission. Institutional leaders, faculty developers, and faculty members could then make thoughtful decisions together about how faculty members can be best supported in their work in ways that enhance faculty satisfaction and institutional goals. If institutions recognize developers' expertise in these areas, faculty development will be well positioned to support not only individual faculty development but also institutional decision-making. Faculty development will be far from marginal and optional. From a strategic leadership perspective, it will be a key lever for ensuring institutional quality, responsiveness, creativity, and excellence. Nevertheless, this broadening of focus should not be promoted at the expense of individual faculty members. As one developer reminded us, "Real change begins with individuals so that work should not be neglected."

Questions for Consideration

• What are the goals of your faculty development program and to what degree do they encompass the critical needs of both individual faculty members and the institution?

• Where are the gaps in how your faculty development program supports individual faculty members' needs and the communal good of the institution?

• To what extent does your institution's strategic planning address faculty development as a critical factor in efforts to enhance individual faculty development and institutional performance?

• How can your faculty development program help to balance the need for assessment used for personnel decision-making or accountability with assessment used for the improvement of teaching and learning?

• In what ways can your faculty development program help departments, colleges, and the institution examine and improve faculty evaluation policies and practices, particularly the evaluation of teaching?

Context still matters

One of the distinguishing characteristics of American higher education is the diverse array of institutional types available to educate students and to serve the nation's needs. What this institutional diversity implies is that faculty work is not the same everywhere. What institutions value and faculty members need with regard to faculty development will therefore vary somewhat. Our study validated what developers already knew: faculty development plans cannot be generic, nor is a single vision for faculty development for the coming years appropriate.

It is important to note that there are core goals that are common to faculty development programs across all institutional types—creating a culture of teaching excellence, responding to individual faculty members' needs, advancing new initiatives in teaching and learning. Yet it is clear that faculty development modes, structures, influences on practice, and current and future priorities vary considerably by institutional type, with community colleges having the most distinctive differences. We also found that the most widely recognized models and shared practices tended to come from large research universities. We hope that our exploration of differences by institutional type, the growth of networks by institutional type, and the impact of the Hesburgh Awards, which are wide-ranging across types of institutions, will suggest new models. In the future, we will need exemplars of effective faculty development programs and strategies from the widest range of institutional types. The excellence of any program will continue to depend on the culture, missions, and needs of the particular institution and the extent to which the faculty development program matches that situation.

Questions for Consideration

- What goals and outcomes do you wish to achieve through faculty development for your institution and for your particular group of faculty members and academic leaders?

- What challenges and opportunities pertaining to faculty development has the institution encountered in the past that should be considered in planning and addressing your particular needs?

- What are the key aspects of your institutional culture and mission that should be considered in planning faculty development that addresses the needs of your faculty members and institution?

- How can you best collect feedback from various stakeholders on what are the top issues facing your faculty and institution?

- How can your faculty development program help collect such information and address key issues through appropriate services?

Redefine faculty diversity

While faculty development programs must find ways to achieve economies of scale and meet multiple goals in efficient ways, a one-size-fits-all model does not meet all needs. Faculty developers already share a commitment to the principle of honoring faculty diversity. Effective faculty development programs have long recognized that faculty have different needs at different stages of their careers, and, in response, these programs have created initiatives to address a range of differing interests and to encompass as many faculty members as possible.

Our study found high interest among developers in mentoring and supporting the most recent and diverse newcomers to faculty. In addition, developers were concerned about the needs of faculty in new appointment types—nontenure-track, part-time, and adjunct roles. There was also recognition of the need for leadership training for faculty who take on department chair positions, and, at research universities, in supporting graduate students as they travel on a path to the professoriate. Working with a more sophisticated definition of faculty diversity will be increasingly important for the field of faculty development. The challenge will become how to meet this principle within the bounds of human and financial resources—for example, some institutions have only one faculty developer. An excellent faculty development plan, organized as a strategic institutional resource, may need to prioritize the needs and requirements of different groups of faculty members.

Questions for Consideration

- To what extent do you serve the various types of faculty members through your institution's faculty development offerings (e.g., early, mid-career, or senior faculty; tenure-stream or tenured faculty; non-tenure-stream or term appointment faculty; faculty of color; international faculty; department chairs)?
- Are you providing enough services for part-time and adjunct faculty? For graduate student instructors?

- To what extent is faculty development offered at various times and in various forms (e.g., short-term versus long-term programs; different times of day or evening; during the semester versus before or after the semester)?

- To what extent does your faculty development program provide opportunities for faculty to explore together interdisciplinary and collaborative teaching and learning experiences?

- How can your institution provide all of its instructors with knowledge, skills, and values that respect and promote multicultural learning in its broadest sense?

- What implications does increasing faculty and student diversity have for the growth of faculty development associations as multicultural organizations?

Faculty development is everyone's work

Faculty development programs that support the full range of work in which faculty members are engaged will require institutional commitment and collaboration. Faculty developers already handle heavy loads, and it is unreasonable, if not impossible, to simply add on more work. The only answer is to recognize faculty development as an institutional responsibility and develop an institutional plan to meet this priority. Faculty development that is "border crossing" may be offered within or among academic departments or various institutional units, such as an institution's graduate school, research support office, student affairs unit, or assessment office. It can be found in opportunities for interdisciplinary teaching and scholarship, in faculty learning communities, or beyond the institution in scholarly and professional associations. At some institutions, faculty development professionals may be the coordinators and resource people who identify the array of opportunities available to faculty members, publicize those options, and coordinate communication among institutional units offering opportunities. Elsewhere, faculty development professionals may focus on teaching-related support (the mission historically most emphasized by faculty development professionals), leaving to other institutional leaders the responsibility of coordinating professional development that addresses other aspects of the institutional missions. Regardless of the specific organizational structure selected, institutions that will be most effective in meeting both individual and institutional needs will be those that approach faculty development as collaborative, community work—within and beyond the institution.

Questions for Consideration

- Who should be responsible for faculty development and what should be the scope of endeavor?

- What organizational arrangements best fit your institution's culture, history, and needs? A centralized unit or office? A network of opportunities coordinated across various institutional units? A combination of departmental, college-based, and institutionally based faculty development opportunities?

- How and to what extent is collaboration occurring across the institution to provide faculty development, and how could such collaboration be improved?

- How might faculty support services on campus be better coordinated?

- What avenues beyond the institution might be valuable to pursue in terms of faculty development opportunities (e.g., local communities, regional and national higher education and disciplinary associations and consortia, global communities)?

- Does the institution have a plan to assess the impact of faculty development efforts on individual faculty members and on the institution, to use the findings for institutional planning, and to disseminate results in venues that help strengthen the profession?

Concluding Thoughts

The findings of this study validate our belief that faculty development is a critically important lever for ensuring institutional excellence. As the context for higher education changes and faculty members assume new roles and responsibilities, faculty development professionals *and* senior institutional leaders must grapple with the question of the place of faculty development within the institutional landscape. Will faculty development be a useful but marginal resource, or will it be conceptualized and organized in ways that make it central to institutional quality, health, and excellence, and essential to individual faculty members' growth?

The lead author of this book posed this question to about 200 members of the POD Network during the closing session of the annual conference in Montreal (Sorcinelli, 2004). Specifically, she invited the audience to quickly "create a rough sketch of the Age of Faculty Development that we are in, what are its unique challenges and how might developers address them." The point of the exercise was to unleash creative thinking about the future of faculty development, asking participants to go beyond words by creating pictures, simple shapes, or symbols. Developers shared their metaphors and, much like in our emerging agenda, their images were either of faculty developers or the field. The images of developers were often related to the notion of guidance and support—assistance that apparently was met with mostly positive reviews by faculty members. One developer saw himself as a "candle bearer," looking beyond utilitarian purposes to carry light, stir hope, and inspire action, despite "stormy weather" in the shape of "reduced funding, global changes, corporate impact, and disciplinary divides" on the road ahead. Another developer drew herself as a "sherpa guide," knowledgeable about the campus culture and terrain, experienced in guiding many different kinds of trekkers, well-trained in the use of appropriate equipment and resources, and respectful and committed to faculty members' needs and interests throughout the trip. Another developer sketched himself carrying boxes of "new ideas," "new energy," and "new techniques" back to his institution while someone in the doorway of a building labeled "my institution" was peering out and exclaiming, "What is he dragging home this time?"

Many of the developers' images of the future of the field of faculty development were about linkages and connections. Faculty developers drew themselves creating opportunities for faculty and other constituencies to network, communicate, mentor, and learn from each other. One group of developers drew a mechanical gear with the idea that "movement and activity [are] not simply spinning in space but [are] making things happen. This is coupled with strategic knowledge and thinking so that we know what other things are being affected by us and will affect us." Another group drew a large magnifying glass through which "we could examine ourselves as a field." The field itself was a series of interconnected pods, labeled faculty, students, the institution, and the community. A third group drew a Venn diagram illustrating their desire for more visible connections "among faculty development, student affairs and development, and the goals of our institutions." Drawing upon the theme of an earlier keynote presentation, the last group drew a tall silo that morphed into a lush rainforest. These developers wrote about their wish for a future in which the silos vanish and "our faculty development centers and universities become rainforests in which faculty can grow their utopian dreams."

There is much to be hopeful about when reflecting on these metaphors of the future of faculty development. Despite all the forces for change pressing on faculty and their institutions—information technology, multiculturalism, performance measures, competition, globalization, and the ever more rapid pace of academic life—faculty developers are still dedicated to their earliest goal of addressing the needs of the "whole person" in a flourishing campus environment. They are dedicated to creating an academic rainforest that is generative, renewing, based on discourse across boundaries, and offering mutual support, collegiality, and community in every sense of those words. As we continue to envision the future of faculty development, we invite students, faculty members, academic leaders, and all others committed to teaching and learning to explore and enhance this place with us.

Envisioning the Future of Faculty Development: A Survey of Faculty Development Professionals

Please tell us about yourself and your institution's faculty development infrastructure.

1) Please check all titles or roles that apply to you.

    __ Director   __ Assistant/Associate Director

    __ Program Coordinator   __ Technology Coordinator

    __ Senior-Level Administrator   __ Instructional Development
                                                 Consultant

    __ Faculty Member—discipline/field: _____

    __ Other (please specify): _____

2) On the list above, please *circle* your primary title.

3) How long have you held a position of responsibility in faculty development?

    _____ Years—total

    _____ Years—at this institution

4) What is your institution's (1994) Carnegie Classification?

__ Research I or II   __ Liberal Arts I or II

__ Doctoral I or II   __ Community, Junior, or Technical College

__ Comprehensive I or II

__ Other type of institution (please specify): _____

5) Is your institution: __ Public __ Private

6) What best describes your institution's faculty development structure?

__ A centralized unit with dedicated staff that offers a range of faculty development programs

__ A "clearinghouse" for programs and offerings that are sponsored across the institution, but offering few programs itself

__ A committee charged with supporting faculty development

__ An individual faculty member or administrator charged with supporting faculty development

__ Other (please describe): _____

7) Program Goals and Purposes

Faculty development programs may be guided by various goals and purposes. On the following list of possibilities, please indicate the degree to which your program/unit is guided by any of the following purposes.

NS	1	2	3	4
Not Sure	Not At All	To a Slight Degree	To a Moderate Degree	To a Great Degree

___ a) To respond to and support individual faculty members' goals for professional development

___ b) To foster collegiality within and among faculty members and/or departments

___ c) To provide recognition and reward for excellence in teaching

___ d) To create or sustain a culture of teaching excellence

___ e) To advance new initiatives in teaching and learning

___ f) To act as a change agent within the institution

___ g) To respond to critical needs as defined by the institution

___ h) To provide support for faculty members who are experiencing difficulties with their teaching

___ i) To support departmental goals, planning, and development

___ j) To position the institution at the forefront of educational innovation

___ k) Other (please specify): _____

8) Please indicate the three *primary* purposes that guide your program, using the letters from the list above.

   _____

   _____

   _____

9) Program Influences

   Faculty development programs may be influenced by a variety of factors. Please indicate the extent to which each factor below influences the focus and activities of your program.

NS	1	2	3	4
Not Sure	Not At All	Slightly Influences	Moderately Influences	Greatly Influences

___ a) Faculty interests and concerns

___ b) Priorities of department chairs and deans

___ c) Priorities of senior-level institutional leaders

___ d) Priorities of the director or person leading your program

___ e) Immediate organizational issues, concerns, or problems

___ f) Institutional strategic plan

___ g) Your faculty development program's strategic plan

___ h) Priorities indicated in the higher education or faculty development literature

___ i) Other (please indicate): _____

10) Influences on Practice

Faculty developers may be influenced by ideas and examples from a variety of sources. Please indicate the extent to which each of the following possible sources contributes to *your ideas* about faculty development.

NS	1	2	3	4
Not Sure	Not At All	To a Slight Degree	To a Moderate Degree	To a Great Degree

Literature in:

____ a) Higher education

____ b) College teaching and learning

____ c) Adult and continuing education

____ d) Human resources/personal development

____ e) Faculty development (e.g., POD Network literature)

____ f) Organizational development

____ g) Disciplinary teaching journals (please specify): _____

____ h) Other (please indicate): _____

Organizations:

____ i) American Association for Higher Education (AAHE)

____ j) American Association for Adult and Continuing Education (AAACE)

____ k) American Association of Community Colleges (AACC)

____ l) American Educational Research Association (AERA) (specify primary division): _____

___ m) Association for the Study of Higher Education (ASHE)

____ n) American Society for Training and Development (ASTD)

___ o) Professional and Organizational Development Network in Higher Education (POD Network)

___ p) Disciplinary or interdisciplinary associations (please specify):

_____

___ q) Regional faculty development consortia (please specify):

_____

___ r) Other (please indicate): _____

11) Faculty development programs are sometimes influenced by ideas that have been implemented in other institutions' programs. If other programs in faculty development have served as models for your efforts or influenced your program, please list the institution(s):

a) _____

b) _____

c) _____

12) Current Practices

In *column 1*, please indicate the extent to which your faculty development program is *currently offering* services pertaining to each of the following issues

AND

In *column 2*, the extent to which you believe *it is important for your faculty development program to offer* services pertaining to each of the following issues:

NS	1	2	3	4
Not Sure	Not At All	To a Slight Extent	To a Moderate Extent	To a Great Extent

Column 1   *Column 2*

_____   _____   a) Assessment of student learning outcomes

_____   _____   b) Teaching underprepared students

_____   _____   c) The shifting characteristics/demographics of students

_____   _____   d) Integrating technology into "traditional" teaching and learning settings

_____   _____   e) Teaching in online and distance environments

_____   _____   f) Multiculturalism and diversity related to teaching

_____   _____   g) Teaching for student-centered learning

_____   _____   h) Teaching adult learners

_____   _____   i) Active, inquiry-based or problem-based learning

_____   _____   j) Writing across the curriculum/writing to learn

_____   _____   k) Team teaching

_____   _____   l) Scholarship of teaching

_____   _____   m) New faculty development (e.g., mentoring)

_____   _____   n) Mentoring faculty from underrepresented populations

_____   _____   o) Course/teaching portfolios

_____   _____   p) Peer review

_____   _____   q) Post-tenure review

_____   _____   r) Graduate student teaching development

_____   _____   s) Course and curriculum reform

_____   _____   t) General education reform

_____   _____   u) Community service-learning

_____   _____   v) Other (please specify):

_____

13) New Directions for Faculty Development

There are a number of new challenges and pressures on institutions which affect faculty work.

In *column 1*, please indicate to what extent *your institution offers* services/resources pertaining to each of the following issues

AND

In *column 2*, to what extent you think each of the items below *should be addressed through faculty development.*

NS	1	2	3	4
Not Sure	Not At All	To a Slight Extent	To a Moderate Extent	To a Great Extent

Column 1   *Column 2*

_____   _____   a) Departmental leadership and management

_____   _____   b) Changing faculty roles and rewards

_____   _____   c) Training and support for part-time/adjunct faculty

_____   _____   d) Ethical conduct of faculty work

_____   _____   e) Preparing the future professoriate

_____   _____   f) Support of institutional change priorities

_____   _____   g) Balancing multiple faculty roles

_____   _____   h) Community-based research

_____	_____	i) Outreach/service activities
_____	_____	j) Faculty and departmental entrepreneurship (e.g., consulting on behalf of the institution)
_____	_____	k) Unit/program evaluation
_____	_____	l) Program assessment (e.g., accreditation)
_____	_____	m) Collaborative departmental work teams
_____	_____	n) Interdisciplinary collaborations
_____	_____	o) Commitment to civic life/the public good
_____	_____	p) Post-tenure review
_____	_____	q) Faculty roles in learning communities
_____	_____	r) Other (please specify):

_____

14) From the two lists above (Questions 12 and 13), what do you think are the top three challenges facing *faculty?* (You may use numbers and letters, e.g., "12r.")

_____

_____

_____

15) From the two lists above (Questions 12 and 13), what do you think are the top three challenges facing *your institution?* (You may use numbers and letters, e.g., "12r.")

_____

_____

_____

16) From the two lists above (Questions 12 and 13), what do you think are the top three challenges that can be addressed *through faculty development*? (You may use numbers and letters, e.g., "12r.")

   _____

   _____

   _____

17) We are interested in your thoughts about the future of faculty development.

   a) In what directions do you think the field of faculty development *should* move in the next decade?

   b) In what directions do you think the field of faculty development *will* move in the next decade?

18) Please feel free to comment on this survey or write about any other thoughts that occurred to you while completing it.

Tables

Table A: Influences on Individual Practice, by Institutional Type

	All Mean (SD)	R/D Mean (SD)	Comp Mean (SD)	LA Mean (SD)	CC Mean (SD)	Can Mean (SD)	Other Mean (SD)
Literature in college teaching and learning	3.64(.57)	3.64(.60)	3.75(.50)	3.73(.45)	3.63(.54)	3.30(.66)	3.55(.67)
Literature in other areas	3.49(.83)	3.36(.91)	3.78(.44)	3.20(1.30)	3.83(.41)	3.40(.89)	3.50(.71)
Literature in faculty development (e.g., POD Network literature)	3.47(.67)	3.44(.68)	3.55(.60)	3.52(.68)	3.32(.82)	3.46(.60)	3.59(.67)
POD Network	3.41(.75)	3.48(.72)	3.50(.72)	3.37(.78)	3.10(.85)	3.14(.67)	3.55(.60)
Literature in higher education	3.36(.70)	3.41(.66)	3.38(.71)	3.37(.60)	3.07(.88)	3.34(.67)	3.36(.73)
American Association for Higher Education	3.11(.90)	3.25(.85)	3.21(.85)	3.21(.87)	2.70(.94)	2.41(.96)	3.27(.83)
Other organizations	3.07(1.10)	2.76(1.23)	3.08(.86)	3.17(1.17)	3.33(1.00)	3.53(.87)	3.67(.58)

Literature in organizational development	2.55(.88)	2.52(.84)	2.65(.95)	2.37(.77)	2.88(.91)	2.50(.88)	2.45(1.01)
Literature in adult and continuing education	2.45(.92)	2.40(.90)	2.37(.94)	2.13(.94)	2.78(.82)	3.03(.79)	2.41(.80)
Disciplinary or interdisciplinary associations	2.39(1.13)	2.28(1.11)	2.28(1.19)	2.43(1.01	2.84(1.03)	2.11(1.10)	2.64(1.29)
Literature in disciplinary teaching journals	2.35(.98)	2.38(1.00)	2.32(1.01)	2.33(.87)	2.41(1.04)	2.09(.73)	2.22(.94)
Regional faculty development consortia	2.24(1.14)	1.93(1.09)	2.52(1.16)	2.14(1.09)	2.52(1.17)	3.13(.97)	2.38(1.12)
Literature in human resources/ personal development	2.21(.85)	2.10(.81)	2.24(.89)	1.96(.69)	2.66(.96)	2.35(.75)	2.36(.90)
Association for the Study of Higher Education	1.97(.90)	2.07(.93)	1.93(.90)	2.00(.88)	1.74(.83)	1.94(.77)	1.60(.68)
American Educational Research Association	1.85(.95)	2.03(1.00)	1.72(.91)	1.40(.63)	1.51(.70)	2.03(.98)	1.70(.73)
American Society for Training and Development	1.50(.81)	1.45(.77)	1.47(.81)	1.33(.66)	2.00(.97)	1.52(89)	1.55(.94)
American Association for Adult and Continuing Education	1.45(.72)	1.44(.71)	1.45(.72)	1.50(.86)	1.58(.76)	1.32(.65)	1.55(.74)
American Association of Community Colleges	1.34(.70)	1.21(.53)	1.17(.45)	1.16(.43)	2.60(1.03)	1.24(.50)	1.48(.68)

SD = Standard Deviation; R/D = Research/Doctoral; Comp = Comprehensive;
LA = Liberal Arts; CC = Community College; Can = Canadian
1 = Not at All; 2 = Contributes Slightly; 3 = Contributes Moderately; 4 = Contributes Greatly

Table B: Mean Ratings of Important Current Issues and Extent to Which Faculty Development Addresses Each Issue

Teaching for Student-Centered Learning

Total	R/D	Comp	LA	CC	Other
Important to Offer	3.71	3.66	3.68	3.68	3.57
Mean 3.69/SD (.66)	(.63)	(.68)	(.64)	(.57)	(1.08)
Currently Offering	3.30	3.11	3.15	3.20	3.25
Mean 3.25/SD (.92)	(.95)	(.97)	(.96)	(.81)	(.79)

New Faculty Development

Total	R/D	Comp	LA	CC	Other
Important to Offer	3.59	3.64	3.64	3.66	3.59
Mean 3.60/SD (.70)	(.75)	(.71)	(.53)	(.69)	(.59)
Currently Offering	2.90	3.24	3.09	3.10	2.90
Mean 3.03/SD (1.0)	(1.02)	(.95)	(.96)	(1.07)	(.83)

Integrating Technology Into "Traditional" Teaching and Learning Settings

Total	R/D	Comp	LA	CC	Other
Important to Offer	3.50	3.41	3.52	3.63	3.62
Mean 3.51/SD (.75)	(.74)	(.89)	(.73)	(.66)	(.59)
Currently Offering	3.27	3.34	3.23	3.34	3.15
Mean 3.28/SD (.86)	(.86)	(.83)	(.96)	(.88)	(.81)

Active, Inquiry-Based, or Problem-Based Learning

Total	R/D	Comp	LA	CC	Other
Important to Offer	3.59	3.47	3.44	3.46	3.52
Mean 3.51/SD (.74)	(.71)	(.82)	(.73)	(.71)	(.60)
Currently Offering	3.16	2.80	2.81	2.76	3.20
Mean 3.00/SD (.98)	(.93)	(1.04)	(1.08)	(.89)	(.77)

Assessment of Student Learning Outcomes

Total	R/D	Comp	LA	CC	Other
Important to Offer	3.41	3.39	3.49	3.67	3.62
Mean 3.43/SD (.87)	(.92)	(.91)	(.69)	(.81)	(.59)
Currently Offering	2.60	2.48	2.38	2.88	2.84
Mean 2.57/SD(1.13)	(1.12)	(1.17)	(1.11)	(1.09)	(.96)

Multiculturalism and Diversity Related to Teaching

Total	R/D	Comp	LA	CC	Other
Important to Offer	3.41	3.30	3.51	3.46	3.24
Mean 3.36/SD (.81)	(.75)	(.93)	(.69)	(.67)	(1.04)
Currently Offering	2.77	2.75	2.65	2.90	2.80
Mean 2.75/SD (.96)	(.92)	(.99)	(1.08)	(.92)	(1.06)

Scholarship of Teaching

Total	R/D	Comp	LA	CC	Other
Important to Offer	3.40	3.48	3.11	2.83	3.14
Mean 3.28/SD (.88)	(.79)	(81)	(.92)	(1.01)	(.91)
Currently Offering	2.75	2.63	2.50	2.07	2.65
Mean 2.57/SD (1.05)	(.95)	(1.07)	(1.05)	(1.06)	(1.04)

Writing Across the Curriculum/Writing to Learn

Total	R/D	Comp	LA	CC	Other
Important to Offer	3.02	3.06	3.45	3.10	3.05
Mean 3.06/SD (.94)	(.94)	(.99)	(.66)	(.94)	(.80)
Currently Offering	2.37	2.58	2.96	2.46	2.30
Mean 2.46/SD (1.05)	(1.03)	(1.12)	(.98)	(1.00)	(1.03)

Course and Curriculum Reform

Total	R/D	Comp	LA	CC	Other
Important to Offer	3.06	2.81	3.04	3.00	2.90
Mean 2.98/SD (.99)	(.94)	(1.09)	(.95)	(1.08)	(.89)
Currently Offering	2.46	2.17	2.42	2.40	2.65
Mean 2.40/SD (1.04)	(1.04)	(1.11)	(.99)	(1.06)	(.81)

Course/Teaching Portfolios

Total	R/D	Comp	LA	CC	Other
Important to Offer	3.15	2.78	2.82	2.76	2.90
Mean 2.97/SD (.97)	(.85)	(.99)	(.98)	(1.14)	(1.00)
Currently Offering	2.73	2.19	2.00	2.22	2.25
Mean 2.46/SD (1.09)	(1.01)	(1.08)	(1.07)	(1.21)	(.85)

Teaching in Online and Distance Environments

Total	R/D	Comp	LA	CC	Other
Important to Offer	2.96	2.88	2.37	3.41	2.86
Mean 2.95/SD (1.02)	(.97)	(1.05)	(1.25)	(.81)	(1.20)
Currently Offering	2.60	2.71	1.87	3.24	2.90
Mean 2.63/SD (1.08)	(1.01)	(1.09)	(1.12)	(.89)	(1.02)

Peer Review

Total	R/D	Comp	LA	CC	Other
Important to Offer	3.03	2.96	3.00	2.87	2.57
Mean 2.93/SD (1.00)	(1.00)	(.97)	(.83)	(1.02)	(1.16)
Currently Offering	2.39	2.22	2.20	2.15	1.90
Mean 2.26/SD(1.06)	(1.04)	(1.11)	(.98)	(1.05)	(1.12)

Mentoring Faculty From Underrepresented Populations

Total	R/D	Comp	LA	CC	Other
Important to Offer	2.96	2.97	2.82	2.76	3.05
Mean 2.86/SD (1.09)	(1.03)	(1.08)	(.98)	(1.32)	(1.09)
Currently Offering	2.00	2.00	1.69	1.93	1.95
Mean 1.90/SD (1.04)	(1.02)	(1.10)	(1.00)	(1.19)	(1.02)

The Shifting Characteristics/Demographics of Students

Total	R/D	Comp	LA	CC	Other
Important to Offer	2.78	2.92	3.05	3.12	2.86
Mean 2.85/SD (1.01)	(1.00)	(1.03)	(.95)	(.75)	(1.20)
Currently Offering	2.21	2.37	1.98	2.59	2.25
Mean 2.24/SD (1.05)	(1.08)	(1.03)	(.95)	(.95)	(1.16)

Teaching Underprepared Students

Total	R/D	Comp	LA	CC	Other
Important to Offer	2.61	2.70	2.76	3.44	3.62
Mean 2.75/SD (1.09)	(1.08)	(1.14)	(1.23)	(.84)	(.59)
Currently Offering	1.77	2.08	1.87	2.73	2.30
Mean 1.98/SD (1.03)	(.98)	(1.08)	(.97)	(1.00)	(.92)

Community Service-Learning

Total	R/D	Comp	LA	CC	Other
Important to Offer	2.69	2.72	2.89	2.88	2.48
Mean 2.67/SD (1.05)	(1.04)	(1.05)	(.91)	(1.00)	(1.08)
Currently Offering	2.09	2.16	2.16	2.29	2.15
Mean 2.08/SD (1.01)	(1.00)	(1.04)	(1.02)	(1.05)	(1.04)

Teaching Adult Learners

Total	R/D	Comp	LA	CC	Other
Important to Offer	2.51	2.63	2.23	3.32	2.95
Mean 2.63/SD (1.07)	(1.05)	(1.07)	(1.19)	(.72)	(.90)
Currently Offering	1.99	1.99	1.69	2.63	2.48
Mean 2.08/SD (1.03)	(.96)	(1.02)	(.97)	(1.07)	(.98)

General Education Reform

Total	R/D	Comp	LA	CC	Other
Important to Offer	2.65	2.53	2.84	2.87	2.52
Mean 2.60/SD (1.14)	(1.10)	(1.21)	(1.12)	(1.18)	(1.12)
Currently Offering	1.96	1.95	2.29	2.20	2.05
Mean 1.98/SD (1.06)	(1.00)	(1.12)	(1.20)	(1.10)	(.94)

Team Teaching

Total	R/D	Comp	LA	CC	Other
Important to Offer	2.57	2.35	2.61	2.54	2.14
Mean 2.49/SD (.97)	(.96)	(1.06)	(.84)	(.98)	(1.01)
Currently Offering	1.95	1.85	2.00	1.83	1.70
Mean 1.91/SD (.87)	(.91)	(.81)	(.87)	(.77)	(.86)

Graduate Student Teaching Development

Total	R/D	Comp	LA	CC	Other
Important to Offer	3.29	1.67	1.50	1.29	1.81
Mean 2.46/SD (1.37)	(1.01)	(1.20)	(1.09)	(1.05)	(1.17)
Currently Offering	2.85	1.28	1.17	.94	1.25
Mean 2.07/SD (1.33)	(1.15)	(.94)	(.86)	(.44)	(1.02)

Post-Tenure Review

Total	R/D	Comp	LA	CC	Other
Important to Offer	2.51	2.48	2.64	2.22	1.91
Mean 2.37/SD(1.22)	(1.21)	(1.20)	(1.16)	(1.31)	(1.23)
Currently Offering	1.78	1.88	1.67	1.58	1.14
Mean 1.69/SD(1.05)	(1.08)	(1.08)	(1.13)	(.81)	(.73)

SD = Standard Deviation; 1 = Not at All; 2 = To a Slight Extent; 3 = To a Moderate Extent; 4 = To a Great Extent

Table C: Mean Ratings of New Issues and Extent to Which Faculty Development Addresses Each Issue

Training and Support for Part-Time/Adjunct Faculty

Total	R/D	Comp	LA	CC	Other
Important to Offer	3.15	3.37	3.04	3.71	3.33
Mean 3.26/SD (.83)	(.84)	(.80)	(.98)	(.60)	(.58)
Currently Offering	1.98	2.20	1.91	2.66	1.90
Mean 2.11/SD (.99)	(.91)	(1.02)	(1.01)	(.94)	(1.04)

Changing Faculty Roles and Rewards

Total	R/D	Comp	LA	CC	Other
Important to Offer	3.28	3.17	3.37	2.90	3.27
Mean 3.18/SD (.90)	(.80)	(.98)	(.69)	(1.06)	(.70)
Currently Offering	2.17	2.25	2.25	1.83	2.14
Mean 2.12/SD (.95)	(.91)	(1.02)	(.99)	(.93)	(.96)

Departmental Leadership and Management

Total	R/D	Comp	LA	CC	Other
Important to Offer	3.16	2.95	3.31	3.15	3.09
Mean 3.10/SD (1.02)	(.99)	(1.07)	(.98)	(1.10)	(.92)
Currently Offering	2.00	1.93	1.80	2.05	1.52
Mean 1.94/SD (1.00)	(.97)	(1.02)	(.94)	(1.07)	(.87)

Balancing Multiple Faculty Roles

Total	R/D	Comp	LA	CC	Other
Important to Offer	3.10	3.06	3.30	2.85	3.14
Mean 3.08/SD (.93)	(.87)	(.99)	(.70)	(1.13)	(.94)
Currently Offering	2.17	2.08	2.25	1.85	2.24
Mean 2.12/SD (.99)	(.95)	(1.12)	(1.04)	(.82)	(1.00)

Interdisciplinary Collaborations

Total	R/D	Comp	LA	CC	Other
Important to Offer	3.10	2.88	3.30	3.07	2.91
Mean 3.05/SD (1.04)	(1.03)	(1.11)	(.95)	(1.10)	(.92)
Currently Offering	2.29	2.15	2.53	2.05	1.76
Mean 2.24/SD(1.03)	(1.03)	(1.04)	(1.18)	(.89)	(1.22)

Support of Institutional Change Priorities

Total	R/D	Comp	LA	CC	Other
Important to Offer	2.97	2.70	3.05	3.12	2.86
Mean 2.89/SD (1.06)	(.96)	(1.21)	(.91)	(1.12)	(1.32)
Currently Offering	2.39	2.32	2.26	2.56	2.00
Mean 2.34/SD(1.08)	(1.02)	(1.22)	(1.00)	(1.00)	(1.22)

Preparing the Future Professoriate

Total	R/D	Comp	LA	CC	Other
Important to Offer	3.45	2.29	2.17	2.46	2.38
Mean 2.88/SD (1.25)	(.88)	(1.30)	(1.14)	(1.45)	(1.24)
Currently Offering	2.75	1.58	1.53	1.85	1.76
Mean 2.20/SD (1.18)	(1.06)	(1.00)	(.96)	(1.14)	(1.09)

Faculty Roles in Learning Communities

Total	R/D	Comp	LA	CC	Other
Important to Offer	2.92	2.79	2.84	2.90	3.05
Mean 2.83/SD(1.14)	(1.12)	(1.15)	(1.02)	(1.08)	(.79)
Currently Offering	1.96	1.90	1.95	2.15	2.19
Mean 1.94/SD(1.05)	(1.08)	(1.10)	(.92)	(.96)	(.81)

Ethical Conduct of Faculty Work

Total	R/D	Comp	LA	CC	Other
Important to Offer	2.72	2.85	2.70	3.07	2.86
Mean 2.81/SD(1.06)	(1.04)	(1.15)	(1.13)	(.96)	(1.04)
Currently Offering	1.76	1.87	1.78	2.10	1.71
Mean 1.84/SD(1.02)	(.99)	(1.09)	(1.02)	(1.09)	(1.01)

Program Assessment (e.g., accreditation)

Total	R/D	Comp	LA	CC	Other
Important to Offer	2.73	2.59	3.23	3.05	2.50
Mean 2.76/SD(1.16)	(1.10)	(1.25)	(.96)	(1.22)	(1.19)
Currently Offering	2.45	2.47	2.71	2.41	2.29
Mean 2.47/SD(1.16)	(1.14)	(1.21)	(1.18)	(1.14)	(1.23)

Unit/Program Evaluation

Total	R/D	Comp	LA	CC	Other
Important to Offer	2.76	2.55	2.86	2.88	2.27
Mean 2.70/SD (1.17)	(1.14)	(1.24)	(.95)	(1.27)	(1.16)
Currently Offering	2.29	2.10	2.22	2.12	1.86
Mean 2.20/SD (1.12)	(1.09)	(1.20)	(1.08)	(1.08)	(1.06)

Collaborative Departmental Work Teams

Total	R/D	Comp	LA	CC	Other
Important to Offer	2.74	2.32	2.55	2.68	2.55
Mean 2.60/SD(1.13)	(1.09)	(1.21)	(.93)	(1.29)	(1.01)
Currently Offering	1.78	1.70	1.78	1.78	1.71
Mean 1.76/SD(.99)	(.99)	(1.00)	(1.04)	(.96)	(1.06)

Commitment to Civic Life/the Public Good

Total	R/D	Comp	LA	CC	Other
Important to Offer	2.61	2.62	3.02	2.60	2.41
Mean 2.59/SD(1.19)	(1.14)	(1.23)	(.94)	(1.22)	(1.30)
Currently Offering	1.97	2.06	2.30	1.71	1.76
Mean 1.97/SD(1.07)	(1.04)	(1.12)	(.95)	(.98)	(1.22)

Outreach/Service Activities

Total	R/D	Comp	LA	CC	Other
Important to Offer	2.44	2.46	2.70	2.55	1.91
Mean 2.37/SD(1.19)	(1.14)	(1.15)	(.99)	(1.22)	(1.34)
Currently Offering	2.04	2.09	2.23	1.88	1.57
Mean 1.99/SD(1.08)	(1.10)	(1.06)	(1.07)	(1.00)	(.93)

Community-Based Research

Total	R/D	Comp	LA	CC	Other
Important to Offer	2.29	2.12	2.41	2.15	1.68
Mean 2.17/SD(1.17)	(1.14)	(1.15)	(.97)	(1.27)	(1.25)
Currently Offering	1.67	1.59	1.87	1.55	1.19
Mean 1.64/SD(.96)	(1.02)	(.94)	(.84)	(.81)	(.68)

Faculty and Departmental Entrepreneurship

Total	R/D	Comp	LA	CC	Other
Important to Offer	1.75	1.63	2.00	1.87	1.59
Mean 1.75/SD(1.14)	(1.09)	(1.18)	(1.15)	(1.28)	(1.10)
Currently Offering	1.56	1.32	1.47	1.28	1.10
Mean 1.44/SD(.99)	(1.05)	(.94)	(.93)	(.72)	(.70)

SD = Standard Deviation; 1 = Not at All; 2 = To a Slight Extent;
3 = To a Moderate Extent; 4 = To a Great Extent

Hesburgh Award Winners: 1993–2004

1993

Winner
Miami-Dade Community College, *Teaching/Learning Project*

Certificates of Excellence
Heritage College, *Faculty Development Program*
New York University, *Faculty Resource Network*
Seattle University, *Faculty Development Program for the New Core Curriculum*
Syracuse University, *Future Professoriate Project*
University of Washington, *Entry-Level Initiative*
Virginia Union University, *Faculty Development Program*

1994

Winners
Alverno College, *Faculty as Scholars of Teaching*
Miami University of Ohio, *The Teaching Scholars Program*

Certificates of Excellence

University of California–Berkeley, *American Cultures Program*

The Evergreen State College, *Washington Center for Improving the Quality of Undergraduate Education*

Highline Community College, Skagit Valley College, and South Seattle Community College, *Highline/Skagit Valley/South Seattle Cooperative*

Johnson C. Smith University, *Faculty Development Program*

1995

Winner

Rensselaer Polytechnic Institute, *Center for Innovation in Undergraduate Education*

Certificates of Excellence

University of Arizona, *Enhancing the Teaching and Learning of Mathematics with Technology*

Florida Community College–Jacksonville, *Center for the Advancement of Teaching and Learning*

King's College, *Faculty Development and Student Learning Assessment*

Metropolitan State University, *Faculty Professional Development Program/Teaching Center Committee*

Minnesota Private College Research Foundation, *The Collaboration for the Advancement of College Teaching and Learning*

1996

Winner
Syracuse University, *Transformation to a Student-Centered Research University*

Certificates of Excellence
Columbia College, *Collaboration for Academic Citizenship*
University of Michigan, *Undergraduate Research Opportunity Program*
Queens College of the City University of New York, *Faculty Development through Freshman Year Initiative*
Virginia Community College System, *VCCS Professional Development Initiative*

1997

Winner
University of Missouri–Columbia, *The General Education Program*

Certificates of Excellence
Prince George's Community College, *The Science and Technology Resource Center*
Rose-Hulman Institute of Technology, *Integrated First-Year Curriculum in Science, Engineering and Mathematics*
University of South Carolina, *The Integrated Undergraduate Faculty Development Program*
Virginia Polytechnic Institute and State University, *Faculty Development Institute*

1998

Winners

Brooklyn College, The City University of New York, *TRANSFORMATIONS: Faculty Collaboration in a Freshman Year College*

Loyola Marymount University, *Growing Together as a Multicultural Community*

Certificates of Excellence

Robert Morris College, *Writing Across the Curriculum: 1st, 2nd, 3rd, and 4th Generation*

University of California–Santa Barbara, *Instructional Improvement Program*

University of Maryland–Eastern Shore, *UMES/SSU Collaborative New Faculty Initiative Program*

1999

Winner

Georgia Institute of Technology, *Alumni-Funded Teaching Programs*

Certificates of Excellence

College of the Canyons, *The Associate Program*

University of Delaware, *Problem-Based Learning*

State University of New York–Stony Brook, *Undergraduate Faculty Development Program*

2000

Winner
Community College of Denver, *Teaching/Learning Center*

Certificates of Excellence
Ferris State University, *The Structured Learning Assistance Program*
University of Massachusetts Amherst, *Building Community: Creating Campus Change*
University of Michigan, *Program on Intergroup Relations, Conflict and Community*
West Virginia University, *The West Virginia Consortium for Faculty and Course Development in International Studies*

2001

Winner
Utah Valley State College, *Faculty Excellence Through Ethics Across the Curriculum*

Certificates of Excellence
Metropolitan State College of Denver, *Bringing Adjuncts in from the Cold: The MSCD Experience*
Missouri Southern State College, *Bringing the World to the Midwest: The International Mission at MSSC*
University of Wisconsin System, *Women and Science Program*
University of Nebraska–Omaha, *The Goodrich Scholarship Program*

2002

Winner
Babson College, *Reinvention of Undergraduate Business Education*

Certificates of Excellence
Indiana University–Purdue University Indianapolis, *The Gateway Program to Enhance Student Retention*
Portland State University, *Community-University Partnerships Program*
Prince George's Community College, *The Book Bridge Project*
University of New Hampshire, *The Academic Program in College Teaching— A Faculty Development Collaborative*

2003

Winner
Indiana University–Bloomington, *The Scholarship of Teaching and Learning Program*

Certificates of Excellence
Miami University of Ohio, *The Faculty Learning Communities Program*
Minneapolis Community and Technical College, *The Urban Teacher Program*
University of Denver, *Sustainable, Programmatic Innovation in Undergraduate Curriculum*
Worcester Polytechnic Institute, *The WPI Global Perspective Program*

2004

Winner
Barnard College, *Reacting to the Past*

Certificates of Excellence
Fiorello H. LaGuardia Community College of the City University of New York, *Designed for Learning*

University of California–Los Angeles, *Freshman Cluster Program*

Bibliography

Akerlind, G. S., & Quinlan, K. M. (2001). Strengthening collegiality to enhance teaching, research, and scholarly practice: An untapped resource for faculty development. In D. Lieberman & C. Wehlburg (Eds.), *To improve the academy: Vol. 19. Resources for faculty, instructional, and organizational development* (pp. 306–321). Bolton, MA: Anker.

Alstete, J. W. (2000). *Post-tenure faculty development: Building a system for faculty improvement and appreciation* (ASHE–ERIC Higher Education Report, 27[4]). San Francisco, CA: Jossey-Bass.

Altbach, P. G. (1994). Problems and possibilities: The American academic profession. In P. G. Altbach, R. O. Berdahl, & P. J. Gumport (Eds.), *Higher education in American society* (pp. 225–247). Amherst, NY: Prometheus Books.

Angelo, T. (Ed.). (1998). *New directions for teaching and learning: No. 75. Classroom assessment and research: An update on uses, approaches, and research findings.* San Francisco, CA: Jossey-Bass.

Angelo, T. A., & Cross, K. P. (1993). *Classroom assessment techniques: A handbook for college teachers* (2nd ed.). San Francisco, CA: Jossey-Bass.

Aper, J. P., & Fry, J. E. (2003). Post-tenure review at graduate institutions in the United States: Recommendations and reality. *Journal of Higher Education, 74*(3), 41–60.

Astin, A. (2004, June). *Remedial education and civic responsibility.* Paper presented at the meeting of the American Council on Education, Tallahassee, FL.

Astin, A.W., Comstock, C., Epperson, D., Greeley, A., Katz, J., & Kaufman, F. (1974). *Faculty development in a time of retrenchment.* Washington, DC: The Group for Human Development in Higher Education and *Change.*

Association of American Colleges and Universities. (2002). *Greater expectations: A new vision for learning as a nation goes to college.* Washington, DC: Author. Retrieved March 9, 2005, from www.greaterexpectations.org

Association of American Universities. (2001, April). *Post-tenure review.* Retrieved October 12, 2004, from http://www.aau.edu/reports/Post Tenure4.01.pdf

Austin, A. E. (1992). Supporting junior faculty through a teaching fellows program. In M. D. Sorcinelli & A. E. Austin (Eds.), *New directions for teaching and learning: No. 50. Developing new and junior faculty* (pp. 73–86). San Francisco, CA: Jossey-Bass.

Austin, A. E. (2002a, January/February). Preparing the next generation of faculty: Graduate school as socialization to the academic career. *Journal of Higher Education, 73*(1), 94–122.

Austin, A. E. (2002b, Winter). Creating a bridge to the future: Preparing new faculty to face changing expectations in a shifting context. *Review of Higher Education, 26*(2), 119–144.

Baldwin, R. (1998). Technology's impact on faculty life and work. In K. H. Gillespie (Ed.), *New directions for teaching and learning: No. 76. The impact of technology on faculty development, life, and work* (pp. 7–21). San Francisco, CA: Jossey-Bass.

Baldwin, R. G., & Blackburn, R. T. (1981). The academic career as a developmental process. *Journal of Higher Education, 52*(6), 598–614.

Baldwin, R. G., & Chronister, J. L. (2001). *Teaching without tenure: Policies and practices for a new era.* Baltimore, MD: The Johns Hopkins University Press.

Barr, R. B., & Tagg, J. (1995, November/December). From teaching to learning: A new paradigm for undergraduate education. *Change, 27*(6), 13–25.

Bellows, L., & Danos, J. R. (2003). Transforming instructional development: Online workshops for faculty. In C. M. Wehlburg & S. Chadwick-Blossey (Eds.), *To improve the academy: Vol. 21. Resources for faculty, instructional, and organizational development* (pp. 160–178). Bolton, MA: Anker.

Bergquist, W. H., & Phillips, S. R. (1975). Components of an effective faculty development program. *Journal of Higher Education, 46*(2), 177–215.

Blackburn, R. T. (1980). *Project for faculty development program evaluation: Final report.* Ann Arbor, MI: Center for the Study of Higher Education: Michigan University. (ERIC Document Reproduction Service No. ED208767)

Bland, C. J., & Bergquist, W. H. (1997). *The vitality of senior faculty: Snow on the roof—fire in the furnace* (ASHE–ERIC Higher Education Report, 25[7]). Washington, DC: The George Washington University, Graduate School of Education and Human Development.

Bland, C. J., & Schmitz, C. C. (1988). Faculty vitality on review: Retrospect and prospect. *Journal of Higher Education, 59*(2), 190–224.

Boice, R. (1984). Reexamination of traditional emphasis in faculty development. *Research in Higher Education, 21*(2), 195–209.

Boice, R. (1992). *The new faculty member: Supporting and fostering professional development.* San Francisco, CA: Jossey-Bass.

Bonwell, C. C., & Eison, J. A. (1991). *Active learning: Creating excitement in the classroom* (ASHE–ERIC Higher Education Report, No. 1). Washington, DC: George Washington University.

Bourne, B., Gates, L., & Cofer, J. (2000). Setting strategic directions using critical success factors. *Planning for Higher Education, 28*(4), 10–18.

Boyer Commission on Educating Undergraduates in the Research University (1998). *Reinventing undergraduate education: A blueprint for America's research universities.* Stony Brook, NY: State University of New York at Stony Brook.

Boyer, E. L. (1987). *College: The undergraduate experience in America.* New York, NY: Harper & Row.

Boyer, E. L. (1990). *Scholarship reconsidered: Priorities of the professoriate.* Princeton, NJ: The Carnegie Foundation for the Advancement of Teaching.

Brinko, K. T., & Menges, R. J. (Eds.). (1997). *Practically speaking: A sourcebook for instructional consultants in higher education.* Stillwater, OK: New Forums Press.

Caldwell, E. A., & Sorcinelli, M. D. (1997). The role of faculty development programs in helping teachers to improve student learning through writing. In M. D. Sorcinelli & P. Elbow (Eds.), *New directions for teaching and learning: No. 69. Writing to learn: Strategies for assigning and responding to writing across the disciplines* (pp. 141–149). San Francisco, CA: Jossey-Bass.

Cambridge, B. L. (2001). Fostering the scholarship of teaching and learning: Communities of practice. In D. Lieberman & C. Wehlburg (Eds.), *To improve the academy: Vol. 19. Resources for faculty, instructional, and organizational development* (pp. 3–16). Bolton, MA: Anker.

Cambridge, B. (2002). Linking change initiatives: The Carnegie Academy for the Scholarship of Teaching and Learning in the company of other national projects. In D. Lieberman & C. Wehlburg (Eds.), *To improve the academy: Vol. 20. Resources for faculty, instructional, and organizational development* (pp. 38–48). Bolton, MA: Anker.

Centra, J. A. (1976). *Faculty development practices in U.S. colleges and universities.* Princeton, NJ: Educational Testing Service.

Chickering, A. W., & Gamson, Z. F. (1991). Seven principles for good practice in undergraduate education. In A. W. Chickering & Z. F. Gamson (Eds.), *New directions for teaching and learning: No. 47. Applying the seven principles for good practice in undergraduate education* (pp. 63–69). San Francisco, CA: Jossey-Bass.

Chism, N. V. N. (1998). The role of educational developers in institutional change: From the basement office to the front office. In M. Kaplan & D. Lieberman (Eds.), *To improve the academy: Vol. 17. Resources for faculty, instructional, and organizational development* (pp. 141–154). Stillwater, OK: New Forums Press.

Chism, N., & Szabo, B. (1996). Who uses faculty development services? In L. Richlin & D. DeZure (Eds.), *To improve the academy: Vol. 15. Resources for faculty, instructional, and organizational development* (pp. 115–128). Stillwater, OK: New Forums Press.

Clark, S. M., Corcoran, M., & Lewis, D. R. (1986, March/April). The case for institutional perspective on faculty development. *Journal of Higher Education, 57*(2), 176–195.

Cohen, A. M., & Brawer, F. B. (2003). *The American community college* (4th ed.). San Francisco, CA: Jossey-Bass.

Cook, C. E. (2001). The role of a teaching center in curricular reform. In D. Lieberman & C. Wehlburg (Eds.), *To improve the academy: Vol. 19. Resources for faculty, instructional, and organizational development* (pp. 217–231). Bolton, MA: Anker.

Cook, C. E., & Sorcinelli, M. D. (1999, Spring). Building multiculturalism into teaching-development programs. *AAHE Bulletin, 51*(7), 3–6.

Cook, C. E., & Sorcinelli, M. D. (2002, April 26). The importance of teaching centers [Letter to the editor]. *Chronicle of Higher Education*, p. B21.

Core Committee. (2003, April). *POD mission statement.* Retrieved January 10, 2005, from http://www.podnetwork.org/about/pdf/missionstatement.pdf

Cottell, P. G., Jr., Hansen, S., & Ronald, K. (2000). From transparency toward expertise: Writing-across-the-curriculum as a site for new collaborations in organizational, faculty, and instructional development. In M. Kaplan & D. Lieberman (Eds.), *To improve the academy: Vol. 18. Resources for faculty, instructional, and organizational development* (pp. 164–180). Bolton, MA: Anker.

Courtney, S. (2001). Technology and the culture of teaching and learning. In D. Lieberman & C. Wehlburg (Eds.), *To improve the academy: Vol. 19. Resources for faculty, instructional, and organizational development* (pp. 232–249). Bolton, MA: Anker.

Cox, M. D. (1995). The development of new and junior faculty. In W. A. Wright & Associates, *Teaching improvement practices: Successful strategies for higher education* (pp. 283–310). Bolton, MA: Anker.

Cox, M. D. (2001). Faculty learning communities: Change agents for transforming institutions into learning organizations. In D. Lieberman & C. Wehlburg (Eds.), *To improve the academy: Vol. 19. Resources for faculty, instructional, and organizational development* (pp. 69–93). Bolton, MA: Anker.

Cox, M. D., & Richlin, L. (Eds.). (2004). *New directions for teaching and learning: No. 97. Building faculty learning communities.* San Francisco, CA: Jossey-Bass.

Crawley, A. L. (1995). Faculty development programs at research universities: Implications for senior faculty renewal. In E. Neal & L. Richlin (Eds.), *To improve the academy: Vol. 14. Resources for faculty, instructional, and organizational development* (pp. 65–90). Stillwater, OK: New Forums Press.

Crow, M. L., Milton, O., Moomaw, W. E., & O'Connell, W. R. (1976). *Faculty development centers in southern universities.* Atlanta, GA: Southern Regional Education Board. (ERIC Document Reproduction Service No. ED129132)

Davies, J. (1995). *Interdisciplinary courses and team teaching: New arrangements for learning.* Phoenix, AZ: American Council on Education and Oryx Press.

DeZure, D. (Ed.). (2000). *Learning from change: Landmarks in teaching and learning in higher education from* Change *Magazine, 1969–1999.* Sterling, VA: Stylus.

Diamond, R. M. (2002). Faculty, instructional, and organizational development: Options and choices. In K. H. Gillespie, L. R. Hilsen, & E. C. Wadsworth (Eds.), *A guide to faculty development: Practical advice, examples, and resources* (pp. 2–8). Bolton, MA: Anker.

Diamond, R. M., & Adam, B. E. (Eds.). (1993). *New directions for higher education: No. 81. Recognizing faculty work: Reward systems for the year 2000.* San Francisco, CA: Jossey-Bass.

Diamond, R. M., & Adam, B. E. (Eds.). (1995). *The disciplines speak: Rewarding the scholarly, professional and creative work of faculty.* Washington, DC: American Association for Higher Education.

Diamond, R. M., & Adam, B. E. (Eds.). (2000). *The disciplines speak II: More statements of rewarding the scholarly, professional and creative work of faculty.* Washington, DC: American Association for Higher Education.

Donald, J. (1997). *Improving the environment for learning: Academic leaders talk about what works.* San Francisco, CA: Jossey-Bass.

Driscoll, A., & Lynton, E. A. (1999). *Making outreach visible: A guide to documenting professional service and outreach.* Washington, DC: American Association for Higher Education.

Eble, K. E. (1972). *Professors as teachers.* San Francisco, CA: Jossey-Bass.

Eble, K. E., & McKeachie, W. J. (1985). *Improving undergraduate education through faculty development: An analysis of effective programs and practices.* San Francisco, CA: Jossey-Bass.

Ehrlich, T. (2001). Education for responsible citizenship: A challenge for faculty developers. In D. Lieberman & C. Wehlburg (Eds.), *To improve the academy: Vol. 19. Resources for faculty, instructional, and organizational development* (pp. 32–48). Bolton, MA: Anker.

Erickson, G. (1986). A survey of faculty development practices. In M. Svinicki, J. Kurfiss, & J. Stone (Eds.), *To improve the academy: Vol. 5. Resources for faculty, instructional, and organizational development* (pp. 182–196). Stillwater, OK: New Forums Press.

Ewell, P. T. (1985). *New directions for institutional research: No. 47. Assessing educational outcomes.* San Francisco, CA: Jossey-Bass.

Ewell, P. (2001). *A review of tests performed on the data in* Measuring Up 2000 (Center Report No. 01–1). San Jose, CA: The National Center for Public Policy and Higher Education.

Fink, L. D. (2003). *Creating significant learning experiences: An integrated approach to designing college courses.* San Francisco, CA: Jossey-Bass.

Finkelstein, M. J., & LaCelle-Peterson, M. W. (Eds.). (1993). *New directions for teaching and learning: No. 55. Developing senior faculty as teachers.* San Francisco, CA: Jossey-Bass.

Finkelstein, M. J., & Schuster, J. H. (2001, October). Assessing the silent revolution: How changing demographics are reshaping the academic profession. *AAHE Bulletin, 54*(2), 3–7.

Finkelstein, M. J., Seal, R., & Schuster, J. H. (1998a). *New entrants to the full-time faculty of higher education institutions* (NCES Publication No. 98252). Washington, DC: National Center for Education Statistics.

Finkelstein, M. J., Seal, R. K., & Schuster, J. H. (1998b). *The new academic generation: A profession in transformation.* Baltimore, MD: The Johns Hopkins University Press.

France, K. (2004). Problem-based service learning: Rewards and challenges with undergraduates. In C. M. Wehlburg & S. Chadwick-Blossey (Eds.), *To improve the academy: Vol. 22. Resources for faculty, instructional, and organizational development* (pp. 239–250). Bolton, MA: Anker.

Frantz, A. C., Beebe, S. A., Horvath, V. S., Canales, J., & Swee, D. E. (2005). The roles of teaching and learning centers. In S. Chadwick-Blossey & D. R. Robertson (Eds.), *To improve the academy: Vol. 23. Resources for faculty, instructional, and organizational development* (pp. 72–90). Bolton, MA: Anker.

Gaff, J. G. (1975). *Toward faculty renewal: Advances in faculty, instructional, and organizational development.* San Francisco, CA: Jossey-Bass.

Gaff, J. G. (1991). *A new life for the college curriculum: Assessing achievements and furthering progress in the reform of general education.* San Francisco, CA: Jossey-Bass.

Gaff, J. G. (1999). *General education: The changing agenda.* Washington, DC: Association of American Colleges and Universities.

Gaff, J. G., & Simpson, R. D. (1994, Spring). Faculty development in the United States. *Innovative higher education, 18*(3), 167–176.

Gaff, J. G., Pruitt-Logan, A. S., Weibel, R. A., & Participants in the Preparing Future Faculty Program. (2000). *Building the faculty we need: Colleges and universities working together.* Washington, DC: Association of American Colleges and Universities and Council of Graduate Schools.

Gappa, J. M., & Leslie, D. W. (1993). *The invisible faculty: Improving the status of part-timers in higher education.* San Francisco, CA: Jossey-Bass.

Gappa, J. M., & Leslie, D. W. (1997). *Two faculties or one? The conundrum of part-timers in a bifurcated work force.* Washington, DC: American Association for Higher Education.

Gillespie, K. H. (Ed.). (1998). *New directions for teaching and learning: No. 76. The impact of technology on faculty development, life, and work.* San Francisco, CA: Jossey-Bass.

Gillespie, K. H., Hilsen, L. R., & Wadsworth, E. C. (Eds.). (2002). *A guide to faculty development: Practical advice, examples, and resources.* Bolton, MA: Anker.

Gmelch, W. H., & Miskin, V. D. (2004). *Chairing an academic department.* Madison, WI: Atwood Publishing.

Graf, D. L., & Wheeler, D. (1996). *Defining the field: The POD membership survey.* Stillwater, OK: Professional and Organizational Development Network in Higher Education.

Green, M. F. (1990). Why good teaching needs active leadership. In P. Seldin & Associates (Eds.), *How administrators can improve teaching: Moving from talk to action in higher education* (pp. 45–62). San Francisco, CA: Jossey-Bass.

Gullatt, D. E., & Weaver, S. W. (1997). *Use of faculty development activities to improve the effectiveness of U.S. institutions of higher education.* Paper presented at the meeting of the Professional and Organizational Development Network in Higher Education, Nines City, FL.

Gumport, P. J. (2003). The demand-response scenario: Perspectives of community college presidents. In K. M. Shaw & J. A. Jacobs (Eds.), *Community colleges: New environments, new directions* (Vol. 586, pp. 38–61). Thousand Oaks, CA: Sage Publications.

Hagner, P. R., Samson, P. J., & Starrett, D. (2003, January). *Faculty roles and rewards: Where does technology fit in?* Paper presented at the meeting of the National Learning Infrastructure Initiative, New Orleans, LA.

Hecht, I. W. D. (2001). Transitions and transformations: The making of department chairs. In D. Lieberman & C. Wehlburg (Eds.), *To improve the academy: Vol. 19. Resources for faculty, instructional, and organizational development* (pp. 17–31). Bolton, MA: Anker.

Hecht, I. W. D., Higgerson, M. L., Gmelch, W. H., & Tucker, A. (1999). *The department chair as academic leader*. Phoenix, AZ: American Council on Education and Oryx Press.

Hellyer, S., & Boschmann, E. (1993). Faculty development programs: A perspective. In D. L. Wright & J. P. Lunde (Eds.), *To improve the academy: Vol. 12. Resources for faculty, instructional, and organizational development* (pp. 217–224). Stillwater, OK: New Forums Press.

Hurtado, S. (1996, Fall). How diversity affects teaching and learning. *Educational Record, 66*(4), 27–29.

Hutchings, P. (Ed.). (2000). *Opening lines: Approaches to the scholarship of teaching and learning*. Menlo Park, CA: The Carnegie Foundation for the Advancement of Teaching.

Hutchings, P. & Clarke, S. E. (2004). The scholarship of teaching and learning: Contributing to reform in graduate education. In D. H. Wulff & A. E. Austin (Eds.), *Paths to the professoriate: Strategies for enriching the preparation of future faculty* (pp. 194–216). San Francisco, CA: Jossey-Bass.

Hutchings, P., & Shulman, L. S. (1999, September/October). The scholarship of teaching: New elaborations, new developments. *Change, 31*(5), 10–15.

Johnson, D. W., Johnson, R. T., & Smith, K. A. (1991). *Cooperative learning: Increasing college faculty instructional productivity* (ASHE–ERIC Higher Education Report, No. 4). Washington, DC: George Washington University, School of Education and Human Development.

Johnson, D. W., Johnson, R. T., & Smith, K. A. (1998). Cooperative learning returns to college: What evidence is there that it works? *Change, 30*(4), 26–35.

Kecskes, K., Spring, A., & Lieberman, D. (2004). The Hesburgh Certificate and Portland State University's faculty development approach to supporting service learning and community-university partnerships. In C. M. Wehlburg & S. Chadwick-Blossey (Eds.), *To improve the academy: Vol. 22. Resources for faculty, instructional, and organizational development* (pp. 287–301). Bolton, MA: Anker.

Krupar, K. (2004). Making adjunct faculty part of the academic community. In C. M. Wehlburg & S. Chadwick-Blossey (Eds.), *To improve the academy: Vol. 22. Resources for faculty, instructional, and organizational development* (pp. 305–319). Bolton, MA: Anker.

Lambert, L., & Tice, S. (Eds.). (1993). *Preparing graduate students to teach: A guide to programs that improve undergraduate education and develop tomorrow's faculty.* Washington, DC: American Association for Higher Education.

Lattuca, L. R. (2002, November/December). Learning interdisciplinarity: Sociocultural perspectives on academic work. *The Journal of Higher Education, 73*(6), 711–739.

Leaming, D. R. (1998). *Academic leadership: A practical guide to chairing the department.* Bolton, MA: Anker.

Lee, V. S. (2004). *Teaching and learning through inquiry: A guidebook for institutions and instructors.* Sterling, VA: Stylus.

Lewis, K. G. (1998). Instructional improvement in higher education. In G. R. Firth & E. F. Pajak (Eds.), *Handbook of research on school supervision* (pp. 721–737). New York, NY: Macmillan.

Lewis, K. G., & Lunde, J. P. (Eds.). (2001). *Face to face: A sourcebook of individual consultation techniques for faculty/instructional developers* (2nd ed.). Stillwater, OK: New Forums Press.

Licata, C. M., & Morreale, J. C. (Eds.). (2002). *Post-tenure faculty review and renewal: Experienced voices.* Washington, DC: American Association for Higher Education.

Lieberman, D. A., & Guskin, A. E. (2003). The essential role of faculty development in new higher education models. In C. M. Wehlburg & S. Chadwick-Blossey (Eds.), *To improve the academy: Vol. 21. Resources for faculty, instructional, and organizational development* (pp. 257–272). Bolton, MA: Anker.

Lincoln, Y. S. (1999, April). *Seeking a new discourse for the professoriate: Is change possible?* Charles De Garmo Lecture presented at the American Educational Research Association, Montreal, Canada.

Lucas, A. F. (1994). *Strengthening departmental leadership: A team-building guide for chairs in colleges and universities.* San Francisco, CA: Jossey-Bass.

Lucas, A. F. (2002). Increase your effectiveness in the organization: Work with department chairs. In K. H. Gillespie, L. R. Hilsen, & E. C. Wadsworth (Eds.), *A guide to faculty development: Practical advice, examples, and resources* (pp. 157–166). Bolton, MA: Anker.

Lucas, A. F., & Associates. (2000). *Leading academic change: Essential roles for department chairs.* San Francisco, CA: Jossey-Bass.

Lunde, J. P., & Healy, M. M. (2002). A guide to faculty development committees: Goals, structures, and practices. In K. H. Gillespie, L. R. Hilsen, & E. C. Wadsworth (Eds.), *A guide to faculty development: Practical advice, examples, and resources* (pp. 250–272). Bolton, MA: Anker.

Lynton, E. A. (1995). *Making the case for professional service.* Washington, DC: American Association for Higher Education.

Lyons, R. E. (2003). *Success strategies for adjunct faculty.* Boston, MA: Allyn & Bacon.

Mancuso, S. (2001, Spring). Adult-centered practices: Benchmarking study in higher education. *Innovative Higher Education, 25*(3), 165–182.

Mathis, B. C. (1982). Faculty development. In H. E. Mitzel (Ed.), *Encyclopedia of educational research* (5th ed., pp. 646–655). New York, NY: Free Press.

McKeachie, W. J. (2002). *McKeachie's teaching tips: Strategies, research and theory for college and university teachers* (11th ed.). Boston, MA: Houghton Mifflin.

McKinney, K. (2004) The scholarship of teaching and learning: Past lessons, current challenges, and future visions. In C. M. Wehlburg & S. Chadwick-Blossey (Eds.), *To improve the academy: Vol. 22. Resources for faculty, instructional, and organizational development* (pp. 3–19). Bolton, MA: Anker.

Menges, R. J., & Associates (1999). *Faculty in new jobs: A guide to settling in, becoming established, and building institutional support.* San Francisco, CA: Jossey-Bass.

Menges, R. J., & Mathis, B. C. (1988). *Key resources on teaching, learning, curriculum, and faculty development: A guide to the higher education literature.* San Francisco, CA: Jossey-Bass.

Menges, R. J., Weimer, M., & Associates (1996). *Teaching on solid ground: Using scholarship to improve practice.* San Francisco, CA: Jossey-Bass.

Michaelsen, L. K., Knight, A. B., & Fink, L. D. (2002). *Team-based learning: A transformative use of small groups.* Westport, CT: Praeger.

Millis, B. J., & Cottell, P. G., Jr. (1998). *Cooperative learning for higher education faculty.* Phoenix, AZ: American Council on Education and Oryx Press.

Morphew, C. C. (2002). A rose by any other name: Which colleges became universities. *Review of Higher Education, 25*(2), 207–223.

Murray, J. P. (2002). The current state of faculty development in two-year colleges. In C. L. Outcalt (Ed.), *New directions for teaching and learning: No. 118. Community college faculty: Characteristics, practices, and challenges* (pp. 89–97). San Francisco, CA: Jossey-Bass.

National Commission on Excellence in Education. (1983). *A nation at risk: The imperative for educational reform.* Washington, DC: U.S. Department of Education.

Nelsen, W. C., & Siegel, M. E. (1980). *Effective approaches to faculty development.* Washington, DC: Association of American Colleges.

Newman, F., Couturier, L., & Scurry, J. (2004). *The future of higher education: Rhetoric, reality, and the risks of the market.* San Francisco, CA: Jossey-Bass.

Nyquist, J. D., Woodford, B. J., & Rogers, D. L. (2004). Re-envisioning the Ph.D.: A challenge for the twenty-first century. In D. H. Wulff & A. E. Austin (Eds.), *Paths to the professoriate: Strategies for enriching the preparation of future faculty* (pp. 194–216). San Francisco, CA: Jossey-Bass.

O'Banion, T. (1972). *Teachers for tomorrow: Staff development in the community junior college.* Tucson, AZ: University of Arizona Press.

O'Meara, K. A. (2003). Believing is seeing: The influence of beliefs and expectations on post-tenure review in one state system. *Review of Higher Education, 27*(1), 17–43.

Ouellett, M. L., & Sorcinelli, M. D. (1995). Teaching and learning in the diverse classroom: A faculty and TA partnership program. In E. Neal & L. Richlin (Eds.), *To improve the academy: Vol. 14. Resources for faculty, instructional, and organizational development* (pp. 205–217). Stillwater, OK: New Forums Press.

Ouellett, M. L., & Stanley, C. A. (2004). Fostering diversity in a faculty development organization. In C. M. Wehlburg & S. Chadwick-Blossey (Eds.), *To improve the academy: Vol. 22. Resources for faculty, instructional, and organizational development* (pp. 206–225). Bolton, MA: Anker.

Palmer, P. J. (1998). *The courage to teach: Exploring the inner landscape of a teacher's life.* San Francisco, CA: Jossey-Bass.

Peterson, M. W., & Dill, D. D. (1997). Understanding the competitive environment of the postsecondary knowledge industry. In M. W. Peterson, D. D. Dill, L. A. Mets, & Associates (Eds.), *Planning and management for a changing environment: A handbook on redesigning postsecondary institutions* (pp. 1–29). San Francisco, CA: Jossey-Bass.

Pew Higher Education Roundtable. (1996). Double Agent. *Policy Perspectives, 6*(3), 1–12.

Pruitt-Logan, A. S., & Gaff, J. G. (2004). Preparing future faculty: Changing the culture of doctoral education. In D. H. Wulff & A. E. Austin (Eds.), *Paths to the professoriate: Strategies for enriching the preparation of future faculty* (pp. 177–194). San Francisco, CA: Jossey-Bass.

Regents of the University of Michigan. (1997–2005). *Admissions lawsuits.* Retrieved March 10, 2005, from the University of Michigan web site: http://www.umich.edu/~urel/admissions/research/

Reynolds, C. (2003). Undergraduate students as collaborators in building student learning communities. In C. M. Wehlburg & S. Chadwick-Blossey (Eds.), *To improve the academy: Vol. 21. Resources for faculty, instructional, and organizational development* (pp. 225–237). Bolton, MA: Anker.

Rice, R. E. (1996). *Making a place for the new American scholar force.* Washington, DC: American Association for Higher Education.

Rice, R. E., & Sorcinelli, M. D. (2002). Can the tenure process be improved? In R. P. Chait (Ed.), *The questions of tenure* (pp. 101–124). Cambridge, MA: Harvard University Press.

Rice, R. E., Sorcinelli, M. D., & Austin, A. E. (2000). *Heeding new voices: Academic careers for a new generation.* Washington, DC: American Association for Higher Education.

Robinson, B., & Schaible, R. M. (1995, Spring). Collaborative teaching: Reaping the benefits. *College Teaching, 43*(2), 57–59.

Rutherford, L. H. (2002). Factoring out fear: Making technology into child's play with fundamentals. In K. H. Gillespie, L. R. Hilsen, & E. C. Wadsworth (Eds.), *A guide to faculty development: Practical advice, examples, and resources* (pp. 194–213). Bolton, MA: Anker.

Schuster, J. H., Wheeler, D. W., & Associates. (1990). *Enhancing faculty careers: Strategies for development and renewal.* San Francisco, CA: Jossey-Bass.

Seldin, P. (2000, January/February). Teaching portfolios: A positive appraisal. *Academe, 86*(1), 37–44.

Seldin, P. (2004). *The teaching portfolio: A practical guide to improved performance and promotion/tenure decisions* (3rd ed.). Bolton, MA: Anker.

Seldin, P., & Associates. (1990). *How administrators can improve teaching: Moving from talk to action in higher education.* San Francisco, CA: Jossey-Bass.

Sell, G. R. (2002). *A summary of responses to questions regarding the POD futures strategy*. President's report to the Core Committee of the Professional and Organizational Development Network in Higher Education. Retrieved March 22, 2005, from http://adc.smsu.edu/pod/Documents.htm

Senge (1990). *The fifth discipline: The art and practice of the learning organization*. New York, NY: Doubleday.

Shih, M., & Sorcinelli, M. D. (2000). TEACHnology: Linking teaching and technology in faculty development. In M. Kaplan & D. Lieberman (Eds.), *To improve the academy: Vol. 18. Resources for faculty, instructional, and organizational development* (pp. 151–163). Bolton, MA: Anker.

Shore, B. M., Foster, S. F., Knapper, C. K., Nadeau, G. G., Neill, N., Sim, V. W., & with the help of faculty members of the Centre for Teaching and Learning Services, McGill University. (1986). *The teaching dossier: A guide to its preparation and use* (Rev. ed.). Ottawa, ON: Canadian Association of University Teachers.

Shulman, L. S. (2000). *Fostering a scholarship of teaching and learning*. Paper presented at the 10th annual Louise McBee Lecture, University of Georgia, Athens, GA.

Simpson, R. D., & Jackson, W. K. (1990). A multidimensional, holistic approach to faculty renewal. In J. H. Schuster and D. W. Wheeler (Eds.), *Enhancing faculty careers: Strategies for development and renewal* (pp. 167–187). San Francisco, CA: Jossey-Bass.

Smith, B. L. (1994). Team teaching methods. In K. M. Prichard & R. M. Sawyer (Eds), *Handbook of college teaching: Theory and applications* (pp. 127–137). Westport, CT: Greenwood Press.

Smith, B. L., & McCann, J. (Eds.). (2001). *Reinventing ourselves: Interdisciplinary education, collaborative learning, and experimentation in higher education.* Bolton, MA: Anker.

Sorcinelli, M. D. (2000). *Principles of good practice: Supporting early career faculty.* Washington, DC: American Association for Higher Education.

Sorcinelli, M. D. (2002). Ten principles of good practice in creating and sustaining teaching and learning centers. In K. H. Gillespie, L. R. Hilsen, & E. C. Wadsworth (Eds.), *A guide to faculty development: Practical advice, examples, and resources* (pp. 9–23). Bolton, MA: Anker.

Sorcinelli, M. D. (2004). *Envisioning the future of faculty development.* Plenary address presented at the 29th annual conference of the Professional and Organizational Development Network in Higher Education, Montreal, Québec.

Sorcinelli, M. D., & Aitken, N. D. (1995). Improving teaching: Academic leaders and faculty developers as partners. In W. A. Wright & Associates, *Teaching improvement practices: Successful strategies for higher education* (pp. 311–324). Bolton, MA: Anker.

Sorcinelli, M. D., & Austin, A. E. (Eds.). (1992). *New directions for teaching and learning: No. 50. Developing new and junior faculty.* San Francisco, CA: Jossey-Bass.

Sorcinelli, M. D., & Elbow, P. (Eds.). (1997). *New directions for teaching and learning: No. 69. Writing to learn: Strategies for assigning and responding to writing across the disciplines.* San Francisco, CA: Jossey-Bass.

Sorcinelli, M. D., Austin, A. E., & Wulff, D. (2003). *Envisioning effective approaches to evaluating faculty development programs.* Session presented at the 28th annual conference of the Professional and Organizational Development Network in Higher Education, Denver, CO.

Stanley, C. A. (2002). Conceptualizing, designing, and implementing multicultural faculty development activities. In K. H. Gillespie, L. R. Hilsen, & E. C. Wadsworth (Eds.), *A guide to faculty development: Practical advice, examples, and resources* (pp. 194–213). Bolton, MA: Anker.

Stanley, C. A., & Ouellett, M. L. (2000). On the path: POD as a multicultural organization. In M. Kaplan & D. Lieberman (Eds.), *To improve the academy: Vol. 18. Resources for faculty, instructional, and organizational development* (pp. 38–54). Bolton, MA: Anker.

Stark, J. S., & Lattuca, L. R. (1996). *Shaping the college curriculum: Academic plans in action.* Boston, MA: Allyn & Bacon.

Stassen, M. L., Doherty, K., & Poe, M. (2001). *COURSE-based review and assessment: Methods for understanding student learning.* Amherst, MA: University of Massachusetts Amherst, Office of Academic Planning and Assessment.

Stassen, M., & Sorcinelli, M. D. (2001). Making assessment matter: Effective assessment can indeed inform teaching and learning. *NEA Higher Education Advocate, 18*(4), 5–8.

Study Group on the Conditions of Excellence in American Higher Education. (1984). *Involvement in learning: Realizing the potential of American higher education*. Washington, DC: U.S. Department of Education, National Institute of Education.

Sutherland, T. E., & Bonwell, C. C. (1996). *New directions for teaching and learning: No. 67. Using active learning in college classes: A range of options for faculty*. San Francisco, CA: Jossey-Bass.

Svinicki, M. D. (1998). Divining the future of faculty development: Five hopeful signs and one caveat. In M. Kaplan (Ed.), *To improve the academy: Vol. 17. Resources for faculty, instructional, and organizational development* (pp. 3–14). Stillwater, OK: New Forums Press.

Tiberius, R. G. (2002). A brief history of educational development: Implications for teachers and developers. In D. Lieberman & C. Wehlburg (Eds.), *To improve the academy: Vol. 20. Resources for faculty, instructional, and organizational development* (pp. 20–37). Bolton, MA: Anker.

Tierney, W. G., & Bensimon, E. M. (1996). *Promotion and tenure: Community and socialization in academe*. Albany, NY: State University of New York Press.

Toombs, W. (1975). A three-dimensional view of faculty development. *Journal of Higher Education, 46*(6), 701–717.

Trower, C. A. (Ed.). (2000). *Policies on faculty appointment: Standard practices and unusual arrangements*. Bolton, MA: Anker.

Wadsworth, E. C. (Ed.). (1988). *A handbook for new practitioners*. Stillwater, OK: New Forums Press.

Walvoord, B. E., & Anderson, V. J. (1998). *Effective grading: A tool for learning and assessment.* San Francisco, CA: Jossey-Bass.

Walvoord, B. E., Hunt, L. L., Dowling, H. F., Jr., & McMahon, J. D. (1996). *In the long run: A study of faculty in three writing-across-the-curriculum programs.* Urbana, IL: National Council of Teachers of English.

Ward, K., & Wolf-Wendel, L. (2003). *Academic life and motherhood: Variation by institutional type.* Paper presented at the 28th annual conference of the Association for the Study of Higher Education, Portland, OR.

Wehlburg, C. M., & Chadwick-Blossey, S. (Eds.). (2004). *To improve the academy: Vol. 22. Resources for faculty, instructional, and organizational development.* Bolton, MA: Anker.

Weimer, M. (2002). *Learner-centered teaching: Five key changes to practice.* San Francisco, CA: Jossey-Bass.

Weisbuch, R. (2004). Toward a responsive Ph.D.: New partnerships, paradigms, practices, and people. In D. H. Wulff & A. E. Austin (Eds.), *Paths to the professoriate: Strategies for enriching the preparation of future faculty* (pp. 217–235). San Francisco, CA: Jossey-Bass.

Wergin, J. F., & Swingen, J. N. (2000). *Departmental assessment: How some campuses are effectively evaluating the collective work of faculty.* Washington, DC: American Association for Higher Education.

Wolverton, M., Gmelch, W., & Sorenson, D. (1998). The department as double agent: The call for department change and renewal. *Innovative Higher Education, 22*(3), 203–215.

Wright, W. A., & O'Neil, M. C. (1995). Teaching improvement practices: International perspectives. In W. A. Wright & Associates (Eds.), *Teaching improvement practices: Successful strategies for higher education* (pp. 1–57). Bolton, MA: Anker.

Wright, D. L. (2002). Program types and prototypes. In K. H. Gillespie, L. R. Hilsen, & E. C. Wadsworth (Eds.), *A guide to faculty development: Practical advice, examples, and resources* (pp. 24–34). Bolton, MA: Anker.

Wulff, D. H., & Austin, A. E. (Eds.) (2004). *Paths to the professoriate: Strategies for enriching the preparation of future faculty.* San Francisco, CA: Jossey-Bass.

Young, R. E. (1987). Evaluating faculty development programs: program goals first. In J. F. Wergin & L. A. Braskamp (Eds.), *New directions for institutional research: No. 56. Evaluating administrative services and programs* (pp. 71–82). San Francisco, CA: Jossey-Bass.

Zahorski, K. J. & Cognard, R. (1999). *Reconsidering faculty roles and rewards: Promising practices for institutional transformation and enhanced learning* (M. D. Gilliard, Ed.). Washington, DC: Council of Independent Colleges.

Zhu, E., & Kaplan, M. (2002). Technology and teaching. In W. J. McKeachie (Ed.), *McKeachie's Teaching tips: Strategies, research, and theory for college and university teachers* (11th ed.). (pp. 204–223). Boston, MA: Houghton Mifflin.

Index